RANGE ROVER

Trevor Alder

CONTENTS

Foulis

Haynes

ISBN 0 85429 534 8

A FOULIS Motoring Book

First published 1986

© **Haynes Publishing Group**

Published by:
Haynes Publishing Group,
Sparkford, Near Yeovil,
Somerset BA22 7JJ

Haynes Publications Inc.
861 Lawrence Drive, Newbury Park, California 91320. USA

British Library Cataloguing in Publication Data

Alder, Trevor
  Range Rover super profile–(Super profile)
  1. Range Rover truck–History
  I. Title   II. Series
  629.2'222   TL2305.R3
  ISBN 0-85429-534-8

Editor: Mansur Darlington
Page layout: Pete Kay
Cover photograph: A pre-fuel injected 1985 4-door Range Rover Vogue stands in front of a 1974 2-door example
Road tests: Courtesy of *Motor, Autocar* and *What Car?*
Printed in England, by:
J.H. Haynes & Co. Ltd

Titles in the *Super Profile* series
Ariel Square Four (F388)
BMW R69 & R69S (F387)
Brough Superior SS100 (F365)
BSA A7 & A10 (F446)
BSA Bantam (F333)
BSA Gold Star (F483)
BSA M20 & M21 (F485)
Honda CB750 sohc (F351)
Matchless G3L & G80 (F455)
MV Agusta America (F334)
Norton Commando (F335)
Norton International (F365)
Norton Manx (F452)
Sunbeam S7 & S8 (F363)
Triumph Thunderbird (F353)
Triumph Trident (F352)
Triumph Bonneville (F453)
Velocette KSS (F444)
Vincent Twins (F460)

AC/Ford/Shelby Cobra (F381)
Austin A30/A35 (F469)
Austin-Healey 'Frogeye' Sprite (F343)
Austin-Healey 100/4 (F487)
Chevrolet Corvette (F432)
Datsun 240Z, 260Z and 280Z (F488)
Ferrari 250 GTO (F308)
Ferrari Daytona (F535)
Fiat X1/9 (F341)
Ford 100E Anglia, Prefect & Popular (F470)
Ford Consul/Zephyr/Zodiac Mk 1 (F497)
Ford Cortina 1600E (F310)
Ford GT40 (F332)
Ginetta G15 (F496)
Jaguar E-Type (F370)
Jaguar D-Type & XKSS (F371)
Jaguar Mk 2 Saloons (F307)
Jaguar SS90 & SS100 (F372)

Lamborghini Countach (F553)
Lancia Stratos (F340)
Lotus Elan (F330)
Lotus Seven (F385)
MGB (F305)
MG Midget & Austin-Healey Sprite (except 'Frogeye') (F344)
Mini Cooper (F445)
Morris Minor Series MM (F412)
Morris Minor & 1000 (ohv) (F331)
Porsche 911 Carrera (F311)
Porsche 917 (F495)
Rolls-Royce Corniche (F411)
Triumph Stag (F342)

Deltics (F430)
Great Western Kings (F426)
Gresley Pacifics (F429)
Intercity 125 (F428)
V2 'Green Arrow' Class (F427)

Further titles in this series will be published at regular intervals. For information on new titles please contact your bookseller or write to the publisher.

FOREWORD

Ever since the Range Rover was launched in 1970, it has been recognised as a cult car, or a status symbol, and has been admired by all.

Its handsome body (which has won numerous awards), lusty V8 engine, long travel coil suspension, and versatile four wheel drive system all lend themselves to give the vehicle its own special charm that makes it equally at home in Knightsbridge or on a muddy farm and able to perform its duties equally well at either of those places, conveying its occupants both smoothly and safely to their destinations.

Despite having been designed in the late 1960s, its shape has aged very little, and growing popularity can be claimed looking at the ever-increasing sale figures. There are now over 150,000 Range Rovers worldwide most of which, I am sure, are still in use. It has been sold in most corners of the globe and in some areas its scarcity has earned it more snob status than owning a Rolls Royce!

Although not designed as a racing or rallying car, the Range Rover has been entered in various worldwide rallies and hillclimb events, always finishing in admirable positions, and it also pioneered the 17,000 mile Pan-American Highway, which stretches down the backbone of America, in the 1971/2 British Trans Americas Expedition. Indeed, this expedition earned the vehicle an entry in the Guinness Book of Records.

This book aims to highlight the Range Rover's attributes and to note its flaws; the latter being included particularly for those thinking of buying one of the still-expensive secondhand examples.

I have tried to show as many early photographs as possible including some taken at the original 1970 press launch. Thanks must go to Tom Barton OBE for allowing me to show these, as I believe they have not been published before. Other early press photographs were loaned by Tony Hutchings to whom I am very grateful. Dave Shephard supplied the photos showing Rover's early attempts at a Road Rover, and the rather unusual 'sporting' shots; my thanks to him. I am also grateful to *Autocar, Motor* and *What Car?* for allowing reproduction of road tests.

Most of the photographs within the book were taken specially by Andrew Morland, and I thank him, too.

Sincere thanks must also go to Tony Stubbings, owner of Channels Golf Course and the adjacent Mid-Essex Gravel pits in Chelmsford, for allowing several vehicles on his land for photography.

I must also thank the following for allowing their vehicles to be photographed, and for being so patient:

Dave Hulbert	(HMC 743N)
Pete Hutchings	(SXC 237M)
Barry Martin	(NHS 400P)
Dave Knudsen	(YVB 175H)
Bill King	(OUD 66W)

St. John Ambulance, Chelmsford, Marconi Division (WHJ 859S) Martin Han de Beaux, (CVC 862T) (Photographed by John West) and Gordon Digby of 'Cowies', Eastern Approach Chelmsford, for supplying the brand new vehicle (C710 GHJ).

Credit must also be given to Brian Bashall and Jim Cooknell, both of the Range Rover Register, for allowing me to publish pictures of their vehicles, and finally to my friend Dave Herd for helping me arrange the photo session and Paula Daw for helping me proof-read!

RANGE ROVER

HISTORY

Family Tree

The original idea by the Rover Company of producing a dual purpose 100-inch wheelbase luxury station wagon was first thought of in the mid-1960s, although there had been other earlier two-wheel drive prototypes built years before. Cross-country vehicles were far from new to Rover, though.

The Land Rover was initially launched to the public at the Amsterdam show, opened on 30 April 1948, only eight months after the decision to start a Land Rover project had been taken! The Land Rover had been designed to act as a production stop-gap immediately after the war. Rover had a near-empty factory on their hands and it was decided to build at this site a four-wheel drive vehicle aimed at farmers.

The concept of the Jeep was studied and a remarkably similar design was produced of similar proportions and capabilities.

The Land Rover's constant success amazed Rover themselves who originally anticipated only 5000 sales per year. Indeed, after only one year 8000 models had been sold and production figures increased further still in following years.

Since those early days, Rover have never looked back and in 1976 the one millionth Land Rover was built. There have been so many different variants of the basic theme across the globe that it would be difficult to list them all, but amongst the most numerous have been pick-ups, personnel carriers, military types, tilting backs, chassis cabs, forward control and crop spraying types. There has even been a hovercraft.

Land Rovers have been sold to most corners of the globe from Rhodesia to China, and Tanzania to Costa Rica, and have earned a reputation for both reliability and durability. They have been made in various wheelbases from 80-inch to an 110-inch (not including specialist conversions) and many petrol and diesel engines have powered them. Hundreds of specialist companies have emerged selling a vast range of extras, some offering total rebuilds of older models giving them a new lease of life.

So why, if the Land Rover was so successful was there a need for a new more sophisticated model? From the outset the Range Rover was designed to be built in addition to the Land Rover and was not a replacement. So, it was in the mid-sixties that Rover realised that a new luxury leisure vehicle was needed as the Land Rover was not really refined enough in terms of speed, ride, comfort and ease of driving.

Concept

The idea of an estate car road version of a Land Rover had been in the minds of the Rover management for many years before the start of the '100-inch station wagon' project, as it was then known. There had been no estate version of any of their prestigious saloon cars, and so it was an all new venture for the company.

The first project had originated back in 1951, after the successful launch of the P4 saloon (Rover 75 and family). Maurice Wilks, who was in charge of design, wanted to narrow the broad gap between the Land Rover and Rover car production. The company could not afford the retooling for a completely new model at that time, so it was decided that the vehicle should be designed on the existing P4 chassis. Maurice Wilks wanted a road car capable of cross-country work and various front, rear and four-wheel drive types were tested. By 1952 a road prototype was built with four-wheel drive and a Land Rover engine; due to its rather angular shape and large glass area it was nick-named the 'Greenhouse'. Soon afterwards it was decided that rear wheel drive only should be used and the project was named 'Road Rover'.

Final prototypes in the late 1950s were vastly different from the earlier 'Greenhouse' model. Sadly, the cross-country aspect had been lost and the prototype turned out to be just a large bulbous-looking car that somehow still looked typically Rover. The estate body had two doors, a split tailgate and large wheels and a window design from a Chevrolet estate car. Several of the prototypes were fitted with the 90 six-cylinder engine and had a 90 inch wheelbase. Production never did get under way and the Road Rover project was scrapped in March 1958.

By 1964, Rover managing director William Martin-Hurst had been to see Carl Kiekhaefer of the Mercury Marine Company of Wisconsin, USA and bought the rights to manufacture the ex-General Motors 215 cubic inch V8 engine. The engine itself weighed just 12lb more than the Rover 2000 unit and measured just $\frac{1}{2}$ inch longer. A major change was made from the American design, however; the cylinder blocks were no longer gravity cast from metal dies with the liners cast in position, but were sand cast and the cast cylinder liners were then pressed into position. Never before had the Rover Company manufactured such a large engine. It was torquey at low speeds (which increases reliability) and had ample power throughout the rev range. 750,000 V8 engines had already been installed in the Buick Special/Pontiac Tempest and Oldsmobile F85 Cutlass vehicles in the USA, but it was replaced there by a bigger cast iron motor. The V8 first appeared in the UK in October 1967 in the Rover P5.

A year later, the Rover Company market research section carried out a survey and realised from the results that the demand for 4X4 leisure vehicles was very high (especially in the USA and Europe), and that 70% of the 4X4 vehicles in the USA alone were being sold to the private sector.

So, the concept of the Range Rover was born from this market survey. However, Rover knew that the UK market was not used to four-wheel drive vehicles, and so when the original designs were started the vehicle had to be aesthetically acceptable to the ordinary car buyer. Rover knew that in the past, 4X4's were expensive and offered little in the way of creature comforts, and so a compromise had to be found.

The wheelbase of the new design, again named Road-Rover, was set at 100 inches. A lot more research had been done on suspension by this time, since Tom Barton, head of development, had already been trying to adapt the Land Rover chassis to independent suspension. Of course, the final production Range Rover does not have independent suspension but such items as long travel coil springs and a self levelling rear (needed for a vehicle with soft springs and a high

payload) had been looked at. The ex-Buick V8 engine fitted the bill perfectly because it produced the power that the all-new vehicle would need. So with the suspension being finalised and a new engine at hand, the rest of the new '100-inch station wagon' design was started.

Design

Towards the end of 1966, the Rover styling department were busy. They were working on a coupé version of an Alvis and the Rover P6BS/P9 sports coupé and so could not take on the task of designing a body for the 100-inch station wagon. So Spencer King and Gordon Bashford, of the engineering department, set about the project. Substantial funds were available this time, so money was spent on new body tooling. More emphasis could be placed on the shape than ever before so the new vehicle was to use pressed aluminium alloy and steel outer panels.

Both quarter and full size clay models of the proposed designs were made. The first quarter size scale model featured only one waist line along each side, had integrated bumpers, and small round Land Rover-type indicator, side and tail lamps. For such an early model, it was a very good representation of what the finished item was to look like.

After finalising the design, tooling up for the job of building running prototypes began in late 1966 and eventually two vehicles were completed by the latter half of 1967. They were finished in grey and mid-blue, the latter being left-hand drive. Both were registered for the road but displayed no badges. On the first vehicle, the bodywork had two waist lines along each side, Land Rover wheels and tyres, and chrome bumpers. The chrome door handles, typical of the 1960s, were placed immediately below the door windows, but not yet on the trailing edges of the doors as on production models. There were also a pair of similar handles on each side of the bottom of the upper tailgate. The front grille gave more than a passing resemblance to that used on a Minivan with horizontal slats painted the same colour as the bodywork. It was certainly functional! Unfortunately, neither of the two vehicles have survived; they were both scrapped.

Many features had already been settled on by the Rover company and were included within the two prototypes. These included the V8 engine, four-wheel disc brakes with split hydraulic safety system, safety belts mounted totally within the seats, four-wheel drive and four-speed manual transmission with an extra set of low gears, and the sophisticated new suspension system. Permanent four-wheel drive was chosen because it was generally felt that there would be less strain on the transmission (especially when towing) and increased tyre life.

It is interesting to note that at one point a six-speed gearbox was considered. This was designed as a possible alternative to the additional low-speed transfer box but was never accepted since it was felt that a three-position gate would be too complex for some customers, and in any case, the high rotational speed of the gears was thought to be undesirable.

The Leyland/Rover merger occurred in January 1967, and Sir Donald Stokes, Leylands chief executive, was more than pleased with the prototypes. Unfortunately, both the P6BS/P9 sports coupé and fastback Alvis designs were scrapped.

However integrated the new design was, it was felt that it needed some tidying up. David Bache and his design team were called in and more clay models were made studying different styles. Certainly, more than one type of front was considered – one type having a recessed grille and headlamp units. This particular full-scale mock-up featured Rover 2000 wheel trims, recessed horizontal door handles immediately below the windows, a petrol cap behind a hinged panel and rear extractor vents running along the entire length of the top rear three-quarter panels. The basic shape still remained remarkably similar to the original Spencer King design.

Wooden frames were constructed containing studies of different interior trim types. Three rows of seats were considered at one point. The rear two rows folded flat to make a double bed (not unlike that of the Austin Maxi) and there were ashtrays in the rear side trims. The front seats had different seat tip mechanisms but the facings appeared remarkably similar to those on production cars. Cloth trim was also considered; something that was not offered in production form until October 1973.

Leyland (or British Leyland as they were soon to be known) wanted Range Rover production to start as soon as possible (Lord Stokes wanted a brand new model launched every six months) and so the production start date approached rapidly. It did, too, for the Triumph Stag, which was to be released a few days earlier than the Range Rover. Unfortunately, the design team felt that they

could have made good use of another year to finalise interior seating and trim and to iron out any small hiccups!

One point worthy of mention is the aspect of tyres. No dual-purpose, high-speed radial tyre was being produced in the required size (205 x 16) so Michelin set to work to develop one. Dunlop felt it would be too expensive to risk designing a new tyre especially for the new vehicle because production might turn out to be very low. Firestone developed a new size for their famous knobbly Town and Country tyre, so the Range Rover was born with the option of two types of rubber, albeit both tubed.

Production Prototypes & Testing

The earliest pre-production prototype Range Rovers were hand built, under cover, at the Solihull factory in the Easter of 1969, some fourteen months before the launch date. Up to five vehicles were made in various colours (including a left-hand drive example), with black Land Rover style seating and shod with the newly developed Michelin XM&S tyre.

Seven months later, two of these prototypes were flown in great secrecy to the Sahara Desert, West Africa on a proving expedition. The expedition was not without mishaps after the rear axle of one vehicle was torn away from the chassis; this, fortunately, was mended locally. Over 3,500 miles were covered and the Rover publicity film, 'Sahara South' was made. One of these prototypes (chassis 100.5) was later joined by another of the earliest prototypes in barrier safety tests, and both were then scrapped.

Range Rover prototypes were also tested in Europe, and some other hot weather testing was

administered in the USA. Winter testing (probably the 1969-70 winter) took place in both Canada and Finland.

Very soon after this, a batch of 25 pre-production cars was built; they were registered with London numbers YVB 150H to YVB 175H. Most were registered in February and March 1970 although some were registered as early as 2 January 1970 and as late as July 1970. To confuse any inquisitive onlookers they were officially titled 'Velar station wagon' and were badged accordingly.

These early vehicles differed only slightly from production cars. The main differences included: all-aluminium bonnet; a smooth surface dash moulding; lack of instruction plate on the heater; wheels painted Sahara Dust on Masai Red, Lincoln Green and Sahara Dust coloured cars; clock in a different position; differences in seat upholstery; top door trims moulding differences; plainer pedal rubbers; the bonnet prop was attached to the opposite side of the bonnet; front and rear Range Rover badges were metal; and there was no nearside tool box trim cover. (NB. The first 100 vehicles built also had a limited-slip differential and the first 569 vehicles were made with a smaller brake master cylinder. These differences were present, therefore, on the pre-production cars.)

The 20 vehicles used for evaluation by the press (registered NXC 231H to NXC 250H) were registered late in May 1970.

Tooling & Production

Tooling takes huge amounts of money in modern motor vehicle production, and that for the Range Rover was no exception. To reduce costs, however, various components were contracted out to outside manufacturers. Apart from the usual components that are normally made outside a car factory (ie; lights, electrical parts, tyres etc) the following lists the major parts of the Range Rover made by other firms:

Chassis, John Thompson (Pressings Division) Ltd (Wolverhampton).
Self levelling Hydromat strut, Boge.
Shock absorbers, Woodhead Manufacturing Company (Yorkshire)
Pressings & assemblies, Universal Engineering Co. (Staffs)
Injection moulded facia, GKN Sankey (Salop)
Aluminium press work, GKN Sankey (Salop)
Steering, Burman & Sons. (Birmingham)
Fuel tanks, Rubery Owen (Staffs)
Axle housings, Rubery Owen (Staffs)
Wheels, Rubery Owen (Staffs)
Braking system, (Lockheed), Automative Products Group (Warks)
Clutch system, Automotive Product Group (Warks)

Many of these companies were situated relatively close to the Rover factory, thus allowing the shipment of vital parts to be made both quick and efficient.

Production of the Range Rover was a major undertaking to British Leyland since there was no single component shared with the Land Rover. Only the V8 engine was an established major component and only time would tell if all the other parts, once assembled and in use, would prove reliable.

The vehicle was assembled alongside Land Rover production, but certain components were manufactured by British Leyland elsewhere. Transmission casings and bell housings were built at Tyburn Road, Erdington and gearbox assembly took place at the Tyseley and Acocks Green sites.

The actual vehicle assembly was a complicated procedure. Chassis frames were made and to these were added the engines, suspension, running gear, petrol tank, and gearbox. Elsewhere, the body frames were stored in compact containers until required and then assembled together with the upper tailgate and quarter panels, rear side windows, floor, front seat bases, roof, mudflaps, some electrical wiring, headlining and (even at this stage) the interior mirror.

Once the body shell had been constructed, (and already by this point painted) it would be hoisted at about fifteen feet across the factory floor and carefully lowered on to the chassis. Here it was bolted on to ten separate mounting points (these were rubberised to eliminate any squeaking and to take any 'knocks' that the vehicle was sure to obtain during its working life) and all other pre-painted panels (such as front and rear wings, doors, lower tailgate, bonnet etc) and trim parts would then be added and eventually it would be driven off the production line.

Production build-up was very slow, and delivery, it was stated by the factory, was not to commence until at least September 1970. Indeed, only 120 vehicles were registered in the UK by the end of this year. Sales of only 100 per week were envisaged, though repeatedly the factory were told, "You'll not sell them – there's no market."

Launch and Promotional Theme

At one point, it had been hoped that the launch of the Range Rover would occur in 1969. British Leyland were so certain of this early launch date, that they considered entering a team of Range Rovers in the *Daily Mirror's* London-to-Mexico World Cup Rally. The event was due to start in April 1970 (only just after the pre-production vehicles had been registered) but the idea was dropped and a team of Austin Maxis were entered instead. The launch date was eventually set at Wednesday, 17 June 1970 and as mentioned earlier, this was still considered too early by some management staff.

British Leyland wanted to promote the new vehicle as much as possible, and what better way was there than to invite various members of the motoring press to a special launch. Originally it had been hoped to launch the car in North Africa but this idea was dropped in favour of doing a quick 'home' launch in west Cornwall.

The press team was based at the Meudon Hotel, Mawnan Smith, near Falmouth and spent three days assessing the vehicle on a 125-mile course. Twenty vehicles were supplied and were initially driven on small Cornish country lanes to get the feel of them. Then it was out on to the open road and north to Blue Hills Mine, near St. Agnes, a disused tin mine famous to competitors of the Lands End Trail. It was here that many of the early 1970 publicity photographs were taken of vehicles clambering up very steep gradients and speeding across loose shale and heather. Leaving the Blue Hills Mine area, the press had to drive up a very steep, rough track marked 'Unfit for motor vehicles'.

The second of the two special test areas was situated some

fifteen miles North East at an abandoned airfield at St. Eval. British Leyland officials had marked out a handling course here with a continuous set of S-bends to emphasise ride and handling characteristics. The eager press team were also invited to try some high speed, near flat-out, runs on the runway, and at least one vehicle managed an indicated 110 mph one way! One motoring writer commented that the Range Rover could be thrown around like a Mini Cooper!

At the time the Range Rover was launched, British Leyland was singing its praises in press advertisements stating that the Range Rover was four cars in one: A luxury car; a performance car; an estate car; a cross-country car. Who could disbelieve them?

Public Reaction

Even at the launch of the Range Rover, the motoring press were quick in realising the high demand potential of the new vehicle. It was not long before public demand for the vehicle was, by far, outstripping supply. There were three or four anxious people clamouring for each new model built, and the situation did not alter for several years. But why was the vehicle such an instant success?

The Range Rover received superb write-ups in the press in June of 1970. After the Motor Show at Earls Court in October, it received further admiration when British Leyland displayed a stripped down Range Rover chassis and engine which was acclaimed to be the best working exhibit at the show. Immediately afterwards came the announcement that the Range Rover had won the Gold medal for best utility coachwork in the basic price range of £1,000 to £1,750. (The Triumph 2.5 PI estate had

come second.) This award came from the Institute of British Carriage and Automobile Manufacturers.

During March 1971, the Range Rover had come second in Car of the Year run by *Car* magazine. Unfortunately it had been pipped at the post by the new Citroen GS. Later in the year came the news that it had won the Dewar Trophy for 'outstanding British technical achievement in the automotive world'. This was the third time that a Rover car had won the award, and indeed, it was the first time it had been awarded since 1969.

By this time, the Range Rover had even been exhibited at the Louvre in Paris, as 'an outstanding piece of modern sculpture'. What better credit to its design!

By now, waiting lists were as long as ever, despite the fact there had been several large price increases, and it had become obvious that there *was* a market for a luxury four-wheel drive vehicle. The only competition at this early stage was perhaps its 'father' the Land Rover, the very dated Toyota Land Cruiser, a handful of American 4X4 vehicles such as the Kaiser Jeep Wagoneer, and secondhand Austin Gipsy's. The foreign vehicles mentioned were difficult to import and when here, were expensive in comparison. Of course there were other vehicles – large estate cars such as the Peugeot 504 and Volvo 145, but they lacked the off-road capabilities of the Rover.

So the public continued to clamour for them, and the waiting list grew and grew, and so did the price. In June 1974 for example, four years after the launch, the price had risen a staggering 70% to £3,387, compared with for example, only a 34% price increase for a standard Mini 1000 over the same period.

Production Evolution

The general concept of the Range Rover has remained unaltered since 1970. It is a luxury dual-purpose four wheel drive estate car capable of working on a muddy farm during the day, and cruising down to Knightsbridge in the evening, and both with a certain amount of style. It has gained 'snob status' in most corners of the world, as, for example, in Saudi Arabia, where to have a more personalised Range Rover than say your brother, (and there is no limit to what the Arabs pay for conversions) is more important than if you own, perhaps, a Rolls-Royce.

However, let us look and see how production has changed over the years.

It is largely true that British Leyland left Range Rover production alone for the first decade or so. Soon after the launch the public were already demanding four doors, automatic transmission, better interior appointments, less noise and other small creature comforts. But it was not until after 11 years that any of these things were available. True, the first of the major changes occurred in January 1973, but this was really only a trim update necessary after the car's too early launch date as trim specification had not been finalised properly. At the same time however, power steering and tinted glass became options and a much needed rear wash/wipe system was added to the standard specification.

In October of the same year, nylon seat facings, still in the same colour 'Palamino', became an option along with inertia reel safety belts. The upper rear three-quarter panels were to be covered in vinyl not unlike the P6 Rover saloon car range.

In 1975, the 'Option pack' was made available. This consisted of 'Sundym' tinted glass, cloth seat facings, inertia reel safety belts and head rests. It was cheaper to order a new vehicle with the option pack than to order all the extras separately.

Apart from exhaust, and gearbox ratio changes, the vehicle remained basically the same (still available in the same six colours: Bahama Gold; Masai Red; Tuscan Blue; Sahara Dust; Arctic White; Lincoln Green) until the end of 1979 when another facelift, albeit this time cosmetic, was performed. The bumpers were colour-keyed to match the grille in black, side repeater flashers were added to the front wings, halogen headlamps replaced the old sealed-beam units, rectangular door-mounted mirrors replaced the bonnet mounted round ones, and the 1975 'Option pack' was made standard equipment as was power-assisted steering. Two new bright colours were added to the range: Warwick Green and Sandglow.

In March the following year, the seats, still basically the same in construction, were refaced in brushed velour and the front units had a newer type of headrest with a pop-off detachable velvet cushion. Carpet was fitted throughout the car including the bottom of the door trims. A mechanical change to the gearbox was made resulting in the lever having a narrower gate.

It was not until July 1981 that a four-door version was available, and the design won yet another award for its excellence. The rear seats had been shifted back by three inches to give better rear legroom in answer to much criticism. (Two door rear seats remained in the same position however.) There were dozens of other minor modifications, and a major change was the re-spacing of the gear ratios.

In summer 1982, the automatic Range Rover was announced. This used the much acclaimed three-speed Chrysler Torqueflite and provided smooth acceleration perhaps though at the cost of top speed and a higher fuel consumption.

More gearbox alterations came about in July 1983 with the introduction of the five speed. Four speed production ceased, and at last the gearbox was quieter. (Both the automatic and five speed gearboxes could still be locked in to the lower ratio.)

In June 1984 came an almost total update of the vehicle, save for the shape, and mechanical components. The ride became quieter, there was now more modern seating (and the front seats actually reclined!) a new dashboard layout, new colours, and the front quarter-light windows disappeared from the four-door version. Many other changes were made, including an intermittent setting to the rear wiper! A new wiring harness was used and one of many possible extras available was electronically-operated and heated door mirrors. However, the vehicle still retained the same timeless shape as it seems it will for many years to come.

In October 1985, the factory announced the fuel injection Vogue model, a 165 bhp vehicle with a claimed top speed of 107 mph. The model could be distinguished by the new polyurethane front spoiler with twin driving lamps. On 3 February 1986 came the announcement that Range Rovers were to be officially exported to America, under a new company name, Range Rover of North America Inc.

On 23 April 1986 the diesel Range Rover was introduced. It was fitted with a 2.4 litre turbocharged VM engine from Italy. Fuel consumption was reduced — at the cost of a performance loss — and the only exterior change was the addition of a 'Turbo D' transfer badge on the lower tailgate. The diesel model was introduced in the hope that cheaper diesel fuel prices would make the Range Rover more popular in Europe.

Special Achievements

Although the Range Rover has been used in many rallies, including the Paris-Dakar, the London to Sydney (Australia) and various Safaris and Hill rallies, perhaps its most famous achievement was the British Trans Americas Expedition of 1971-1972.

Two Range Rovers were lent to the army to complete the expedition and were extensively modified in preparation.

The expedition was made to bring to the world's attention the need to complete the 18,000 mile Pan-American Highway, which would allow cars to travel the full length of the American continent. It had never been completely conquered before, because there laid a 250 mile stretch of land called the Darien Gap (in Panama), which was a combination of water, swamp and thick jungle. This particular section took 95 days to cross – an average of three miles per day – and fuel consumption was often as high as 1 mpg! Extensive use had to be made of ropes, winches and ladders.

The expedition did not go without hitches, however. On the fourth day, the leading car slid into a lorry straddled across a snow covered road and was very badly damaged. The other vehicle had to tow it 90 miles to Fort

Nelson, where it was repaired by a local Leyland dealer.

In the Darien jungle, the leading vehicle's front differential broke and so all the power was transmitted to the rear. Subsequently, this broke, too, and an attempt was made to tow the lame vehicle with the other. The inevitable happened and the leading Range Rover's differential broke! Failure was thought to have resulted from the large swamp tyres fitted and they were not used again. Rover's chief products engineer, Geoff Miller, had to be flown out to diagnose the problem, and he immediately ordered new parts which were dropped in by aircraft; and progress was eventually made.

The vehicles left the jungle section the day before the rains started which would turn the jungle into an unpassable quagmire. Cape Horn was eventually reached on 10 June 1972, the vehicles having completed over 18,000 miles.

One of the two vehicles (VXC 868K) now resides at the BL Heritage museum in Syon Park, London; the other (VXC 757K) is still used by Land Rover Ltd as an exhibition tow car to this day. It has, however, been extensively rebuilt.

A Success Story

Apart from a slight lull in the market in 1977, Range Rover sales figures have increased steadily each year to a record 13,458 sales worldwide in 1985.

The vehicle has sold the largest number in Great Britain, with 33,487 sales by the end of 1984. Over 3,089 (about 26% of vehicles built that year) were sold in 1984 alone in Great Britain. The Australian market is the most popular for overseas sales, although the vehicle was not available there until three or four years after the UK introduction. I spoke to Greg Pridmore, assistant secretary in the Australian Victoria Range Rover club (which has about 700 members) who bought his present Range Rover new in 1972, whilst he was here in the UK working. At that particular time, the Range Rover was not being sold in Australia, and he had to wait nearly a year in the UK for a car to be available. Waiting lists, of course, were always long in the UK in the early to mid-seventies.

The vehicle is also exported in CKD (Completely Knocked Down) form for manufacture abroad, alongside CKD Land Rovers. There are twenty-three such assembly plants abroad, and sales average 2,300 per year by this method.

Tough US emission control regulations have meant that American customers have never really had the chance to buy Range Rovers until very recently. It was however, originally hoped to start exporting to the US 30% of the total production in 1972!

The following lists not the year by year sales figures, but the total number of vehicles off the production line:

1970	8623
1971	2537
1972	5510
1973	6519
1974	8604
1975	10516
1976	12207
1977	9667
1978	11240
1979	11373
1980	9708
1981	10441
1982	13255
1983	12182
1984	11885
1985	13458
GRAND TOTAL	149,188

Number of vehicles *registered* in the first five years of production.

1970	120
1971	2542
1972	2261
1973	2974
1974	2149

EVOLUTION

Production Changes

The Range Rover was launched on Wednesday 17 June 1970 as a dual purpose, four wheel drive luxury estate car. Only a two door model was offered, (and this remained so until July 1981 with the announcement of the four door) and optional extras offered were few, but such items as a Triplex heated rear screen, a radio, fog or spot lamps and tow bar were available. Six colours were available at the time of the launch being: Sahara Dust; Lincoln Green; Masai Red; Tuscan Blue; Bahama Gold; and Davos White.

The interior could certainly be described as functional. There were no carpets, and the non-reclining seats (something that did not change until 1984) were only faced in leathercloth or PVC as it is sometimes called. The interior could therefore be hosed out after a day at the horse trials or after shooting! One of the many novel ideas introduced by the Range Rover to the automotive world were the safety belts mounted totally within the seats themselves. Rover had to get a new law passed to comply with the regulations on this point. Inertia reel was not offered on the earliest models.

Before looking at all the various production changes that took place over the years, here are the various chassis numbers as at June 1970:

Prototypes:	100.1 to 100.7
Home RH Steering:	35500001A
Export RH Steering:	35600001A
CKD RH Steering:	35100001A
Export LH Steering:	35800001A
CKD LH Steering:	35900001A

1970: Range Rover launched. Note here that pre-production and press vehicles had chassis numbers up to and including: 35500045A.

1970: (from 101st vehicle) The third differential was simplified from limited slip to a normal, but still lockable, unit. By now, bonnets were made in steel, and wheels were painted silver.

1971: (from 571st vehicle) A larger brake servo was fitted.

1972: The bonnet was lightened and the steering box ratio increased from 18.2:1 to 20.55:1 (from 3¾-turns lock-to-lock up to 4¾ to reduce effort). Other improvements were: better gearchange, hub oil seals, body fixings for floor and front wings, improved hinge corrosion resistance, front door hinge mountings, tailgate lock and sealing, rear lamp sealing, and the sharp areas on the dashboard were removed. Opening chassis number for 1972: 35503097A

1973 (January): Rear window wash/wipe system introduced and flip-up petrol cap replaced the earlier screw off type. Interior revisions included carpeted transmission tunnel, cigar lighter, brushed nylon headlining, addition of voltmeter, oil temperature and oil pressure gauges, and rubber sleeve on the throttle. The earlier 16ACR alternator was replaced by an 18ACR unit. Two new options available: Sundym tinted glass and power assisted steering. Opening chassis number for year 1973: 35505287B.

1973 (October): Brushed nylon seat facings, and inertia reel safety belts became two factory options. The upper rear three-quarter panels were covered in black vinyl and the two small metal side badges were altered slightly. An electrical fuel pump replaced the old mechanical unit. The differential lock warning light was resited away from the switch itself to underneath the speedo pod. Door window rubbers were changed and the black alloy finishing trim was discarded from the trailing edge of the rear sliding windows. The upper tailgate gas struts were turned around by 180° and were fitted to the body differently. The air intake tube under the bonnet was changed from a round profile to square. Opening chassis number of new series: 35508190C.

1974: Davos white colour changed to Arctic White. Top of the rear end frame slightly redesigned. A split charge facility became optional for use with the 18ACR alternator.

1975: The vented carburettors were altered and the radiator seals were revised. New vehicles could now be ordered with the 'Option pack'. This included leathercloth headrests, cloth seats, power steering, tinted glass, and inertia reel safety belts. Another interior light was added and better carpet covered the transmission tunnel.

1976: Twin exhausts replaced the single pipe system. The high gear ratio was changed from 1.174 to 1.116:1.

1977: Vehicles could be ordered with door mirrors instead of bonnet mirrors.

1978: Overdrive became an option. The effective step up ratio was 0.782:1. (21.1% drop in engine revs when selected.) Windscreen wipers now finished in black.

1979 (September): Three colours added to the range: Russet Brown, Sandglow, and Warwick Green. Bahama Gold was discontinued. Quartz headlamps replaced the sealed beam units, door mirrors were standardised, front wing repeater flashers were added and the bumpers were now finished in black. The 'by Land Rover' badge on the tailgate was discontinued as were the two small side badges. Transfer strip badging front and rear replaced the old plastic lettering. All items under the 1975 'Option pack' were standardised, although vehicles could still be ordered with manual steering. A fog light warning light was added to the dash as was a brake vacuum loss light. The old three spoke steering wheel was replaced by a four spoke type.

Under-bonnet changes included uprating the alternator to 25ACR (65 amp) and the adoption of a better radio interference suppressor. Air conditioning became an option. Opening chassis number for January 1979: 35552979.

1980: Seat trim upgraded to brushed velour. Revised headrests included detachable velvet cushions. Carpet was added to the leading half of the rear wheel arches, and added to all the passenger footwells. The trim on the bottom of the doors was also improved. A change to the gearbox resulted in a narrower gate. New chassis number prefix starting with: LHABV1AA 100001. The Range Rover Monteverdi was launched in October 1980. This was a four-door version made by the Swiss coachbuilders, and featuring an all-leather interior. Note that the doors were not the same shape as those of the factory four-door. It came in either Green or Silver metallic or Anthracite.

1981: Vogue Range Rover announced. This was an uprated more luxurious model available in attractive Vogue Blue. Map pockets were added to the back of the front seats, and a special picnic hamper was added to the rear cargo area.

1981 (July): Four-door body announced. On this version, the rear seats were shifted back by three inches to give better rear legroom, and the door trim was changed totally. Extras available included electric windows, alloy wheels, and wood door cappings. On all versions the spare wheel cover was now to be carpeted as was the tool kit cover, and rear cargo area. Sun visors now incorporated a passenger vanity mirror and driver's ticket-pocket, and the interior light had a built in delay system. An under bonnet inspection lamp was added and the wipers now had an intermittent setting. Colour changes to the range were the addition of Venetian Red and Shetland Beige, and the discontinuation of the short-lived Sandglow and Warwick Green. Mechanical changes included revised contact breaker points, carburettors and valve timing. A new higher compression engine was standardised (although new models could still be ordered with the old low compression unit) and had a compression ratio of 9.35:1. The engine now used four star fuel. The high gear ratios were altered once again (only to models with the high compression engine) from 1.113:1 to 0.966:1.

1982 (Summer): A three-speed automatic gearbox became an extra, and had the normal manual over-ride and kick down operations. The low gear ratio selector knob was amalgamated with the differential lock knob on the automatic version, and an extra warning light was added to the dash. Four-door options included a rear seat armrest, rear seat headrests and front seat armrests. Tuscan Blue and Masai Red were discontinued from the colour range and Sierra Silver and Nevada Gold metallics were added.

1983: Four-speed Range Rovers ceased as the new five-speed took over. The five-speed box led to a redesigned gear lever and gearbox tunnel console. The exterior door locks on four-door models, were moved up a few inches and integrated into the handles themselves. Central locking was standardised and the lower tailgate was equipped with a torsion bar balancing system to make it lighter. The old mechanical jack was replaced with a hydraulic unit. Two-door models now had windscreen and door pillars in black to match four-door models. The four-door was now available with any one of three option packs. C Pack; armrests front and rear; rear headrests; wood door cappings. B Pack; same as C Pack but with alloy wheels and metallic paint. A Pack; same as B Pack but with the addition of air conditioning. Colour changes once again, were the discontinuation of Shetland Beige and Vogue Blue, and the addition of Derwent Blue metallic. An all-new, even more luxurious, 'In Vogue' model was launched, of which 325 were available to UK customers.

1984 (June): Greatest number of changes made to existing production models since production began.

Four door models: The small front quarter-light windows were discontinued, and new front seats were fitted, which were height adjustable, reclinable, had new headrests and height adjustable safety belts now mounted on the door pillars. Door trims were also revised with built-in radio speakers in the front doors.

All models: New interior trim (carpets, headlining, seats etc.) available in either Silver Grey or Bronze Check. Palomino trim colour now discontinued. New fittings included: larger door mirrors, new dashboard, addition of passenger grabrail, six digit odometer, rev counter, black tailgate capping, tailgate-operated courtesy light, colour-keyed front and rear badging, centre console, revised heater giving 50% better output and hot air to passengers feet, rear wash wipe with intermittent wipe setting, revised upper tailgate struts, new style electrical wiring harness, electronic ignition, side window fresh air vents, new fuse panel, weather shield between bottom of rear tailgate and bumper, and new parcel shelf (not with air conditioning). New major options included electronically operated and heated door mirrors, rear luggage compartment cover, headlamp jet washers, and four way speaker stereo radio cassette system (all standard features on the Vogue model however). Colour changes were:- The discontinuation of Lincoln Green, and introduction of Arizona Tan and Balmoral Green.

1985 (July): Three new colours announced. Astral Silver metallic, Caspian Blue metallic and Chaminix White. The following were discontinued: Sahara Dust (the longest surviving original colour), Sierra Silver metallic, Derwent Blue metallic, Nevada Gold metallic, Arctic White and Russet Brown.

1985 (October): New, more powerful 165 bhp fuel injected engine announced, fitted as standard to the Vogue model. Vogue models also had an all new front polyurethane spoiler incorporating twin quartz halogen lamps. New tyres made for the faster Vogue models were Michelin XM & S 200 x 16, or Avon Range master 215/715 x 16.

The three-speed Chrysler automatic gearbox was replaced by a four-speed auto box, the ZF4 HP22, with a lock up clutch by-passing torque converter in top gear. The manual version benefited from a new direct linkage system giving a smoother gearchange, and a smaller gear lever was employed. 'Roll reducing' suspension was announced, making use of dual rate rear springs, but not to the detriment of the superior off-road ride. Interior revisions included the new central mounting for the radio, and new backlit heater and air conditioning controls. A new cubby box now incorporated a cigar lighter. Vogue models were also equipped with red warning lamps on the trailing edges of the doors (á la SD1) and puddle lamps. New colours announced: Cypress Green metallic, Savannah Beige metallic, Tasman Blue and Cambrian Grey.

New trim introduced: Bracken, which was exclusive to the Vogue model.

1986 (April): Diesel Range Rover announced, powered by 2,393 cc, four-cylinder unit from VM in Italy, and fitted with five-speed manual gearbox only. Heavier rate front coil springs fitted to take the extra 82 kg engine weight, and the additional 12 volt battery required for heavier starting loads. Better fuel consumption claimed: 25.5 mpg urban driving, 34.1 mpg at a constant 56 mph.

SPECIFICATION

Type	Range Rover
Built	Solihull, West Midlands, England. 1970 to date.
Number manufacured (up to end of 1985)	149,188 worldwide, of which 33,487 were registered in the UK by the end of 1984.
Drive configuration	Front engine, four-wheel drive, driven through either a five-speed (1983 to date), four-speed (1970 to 1983), three-speed automatic (1982 to 1985) or four-speed automatic (from 1985), each with a separate set of low ratio gears. The central third differential is lockable for extreme off-road use.

Engine (petrol)

Type:	Water cooled, overhead valve V8. Aluminium alloy block with dry liners and aluminium alloy flat-topped pistons.
Camshaft:	Central position with five bearings, steel-shelled, lined with white metal.
Capacity:	3528 cc (215 cu in)
Compression ratio:	8.5:1 (1970 to 1973) 2-star fuel
	8.25:1 (1973 to 1977) 2-star fuel
	8.13:1 (1977 to 1981) 2-star fuel
	9.35:1 (1981 to date) 4-star fuel
	(Note 8.13:1 engine still optional.)
Bore and stroke:	3.5 x 2.8 in (88.9 x 71.1 mm)
Maximum power (DIN):	130 bhp at 5000 rpm (1970 to 1981)
	125 bhp at 4000 rpm (1981 to date)
	165 bhp at 4750 rpm (fuel injection on Vogue from October 1985)
Maximum torque (DIN):	186 lb ft at 2500 rpm (1970 to 1981)
	190 lb ft at 2500 rpm (1981 to date)
	207 lb ft at 3200 rpm from October 1985 on Vogue model
Carburettors:	Twin Zenith Stromberg type CD2S (1970 to 1980)
	Twin Zenith Stromberg type 175CD-SE (from 1980)
	(Note: fuel injection on Vogue models from October 1985.)

Engine (diesel)

Type: HR 492 HI VM unit. Head/block aluminium alloy/cast iron. Four cylinders in line, wet liners, five main bearings. Water-cooled, with electric fan. KKK K16 turbocharger with air-to-air intercooler.

Capacity: 2393 cc (146.1 cu in)
Compression ratio: 22:1
Bore and stroke: 3.62 x 3.54 in (92 x 90 mm)
Maximum power (DIN): 112 bhp at 4200 rpm
Maximum torque: 183 lb ft at 2400 rpm

Transmission

There are four main types of gearbox: four-speed manual; five-speed manual; three-speed automatic and four-speed automatic. Each gearbox has a separate set of low ratio gears. The differential ratio of 3.54:1 is common to all types.

Gear ratios:	4-speed	5-speed	Automatic (3-speed)	Automatic (4-speed)
first	4.069:1	3.32:1	2.45:1	2.47:1
second	2.448:1	2.13:1	1.45:1	1.47:1
third	1.505:1	1.40:1	1.00:1	1.00:1
fourth	1.000:1	1.00:1	–	0.72:1
fifth	–	0.77:1	–	–
reverse	3.664:1	3.42:1	2.08:1	2.08:1

Overall ratios, final drive (4-speed):	1970-76	1976-81	1981-83	Low ratio (all years)
first	16.91:1	16.08:1	14.34:1	47.83:1
second	10.17:1	9.67:1	8.63:1	28.78:1
third	6.25:1	5.95:1	5.31:1	17.69:1
fourth	4.16:1	3.95:1	3.52:1	11.76:1
reverse	15.23:1	14.48:1	12.92:1	43.07:1

Overall ratios, final drive (5-speed):	High ratio	Low ratio
first	14.01:1	39.01:1
second	8.99:1	25.03:1
third	5.91:1	16.45:1
fourth	4.22:1	11.75:1
fifth	3.25:1	9.05:1
reverse	14.74:1	40.30:1

Overall ratios, final drive 3-speed automatic:	High ratio	Low ratio
first	8.70:1	28.79:1
second	5.15:1	17.04:1
third	3.55:1	11.75:1
fourth	–	–
fifth	–	–
reverse	7.81:1	25.86:1

Overall ratios, final drive
4-speed automatic:

	High ratio	**Low ratio**
first	10.42:1	29.03:1
second	6.20:1	17.23:1
third	4.22:1	11.75:1
fourth	3.04:1	8.46:1
fifth	—	—
reverse	8.78:1	24.45:1

Transfer box ratios:
4-speed manual

1970 to Autumn 1976   High ratio: 1.174:1
Low ratio: 3.321:1

Autumn 1976 to 1983   High ratio: 1.113:1
Low ratio: 3.321:1

5-speed manual
1983 to date   High ratio: 1.192:1
Low ratio: 3.321:1

Automatic
Summer 1982 to October 1985   High ratio: 1.003:1
Low ratio: 3.321:1
(N.B. Overdrive became a four-speed option from February 1978 and when selected gave an effective step-up ratio of 0.782:1)

October 1985 to date   High ratio: 1.192:1
Low ratio: 3.320:1

Chassis

Welded box-section chassis coated with anti-corrosion paint by electrophoretic process.

Suspension

Front: Live axle with coil springs, radius arms and panhard rod. Spring rate, 133 lb in (23.75 kg/cm). (Uprated on diesel models.)

Rear: Live axle with coil springs, radius arms, A-frame location arms with 'Boge Hydromat' self-energising self-levelling device. Spring rate, 130 lb in (23 kg/cm) (Note dual-rate rear springs from October 1985).

Shock absorbers

Hydraulic, telescopic, double-acting $1^3/8$ in (35 mm) bore. Fitted inside front coil springs and each side of axle at the rear.

Steering

Type: Burman, recirculating ball, worm and nut (manual); Adwest Varamatic (power-assisted)

Ratios: 18.2:1 (June 1970 to 1972) Manual steering
20.55:1 (1972 onwards) Manual steering
17.5:1 (1973 onwards) Power steering

Turning circle: 37 ft (1970 – 1984)
39 ft (1984 onwards)

Brakes

Disc brakes all round, servo-assisted. Lockheed four-piston operation at front and two-piston operation at rear, with separate secondary braking system for safety should primary system fail. Total pad area, 49.2 sq in (317.34 sq cm).
Total swept area, 496 sq in (3119.2 sq cm).
Handbrake: mechanical Lockheed 7.25 in (184 mm) dia., 3 in (76 mm) wide duo-servo drum brake on rear of transfer box.

Wheels and tyres

Pressed-steel wheels with polychromatic aluminium light silver finish. (From July 1981 alloy wheels became an option.) Both types five-studded.

Size:
Standard steel wheels: 6.00 JK x 16.
Optional alloy wheels: 7.00 JK x 16.

Tyres:
Michelin XM & S tubed radial. 205 x 16 1970 to date (standard factory fitting) Firestone Town & Country, tubed radial 205 x 16 1970 to date. Goodyear G800 Wingfoot, tubed radial 205 x 16 1979 to date. Michelin XM & S 200 205 R16 or Avon Rangemaster 215/75 R16 (fuel injection models).

Bodywork

Designed by Spencer King and David Bache, originally only available with two doors. From July 1981 the four-door model became very popular taking about 90% of the sales.

Type:
Five-seater estate car with two-piece locking tailgate. Outer panels mostly in 'Birmabright' (an aluminium alloy) except for the bonnet, door pillars, rear tailgate and lower rear three-quarter panels. Outer panels mounted on an inner steel framework.
(N.B. Pre-production Range Rovers had an aluminium bonnet.)

Electrical system

Lights:
12 volt Lucas. Negative earth.
Exterior: headlamps 7 in diameter sealed beam units up to 1979, when halogen lights introduced; mainbeam 60 watt, dipped 55 watt. Sidelights 4 watt; stop/tail lights 6 watt/21 watt; number plate lights 6 watt; indicators 21 watt; reversing lights 21 watt. Interior: roof lamp(s) 10 watt; instrument panel lamps 2.2 watt.

Ignition type:
Lucas coil (BA16C6) with distributor and self-adjusting contact breaker. Electronic from June 1984.
Ignition control: ballasted coil, centrifugal and vacuum advance.

Alternator:
Lucas model 16 ACR 34 amp output (1970-1973).
Lucas model 18 ACR 45 amp output (1973-1979).
Lucas model 25 ACR 65 amp output (1979 to date).
Note that larger alternators were optional.
20 ACR 60 amp from 1975 and 25 ACR 65 amp from 1977.
A split charge facility was optional from 1974.
Note: two 12 volt batteries fitted to diesel version.

Dimensions:

Overall length:	176 in (4.47 m)
Overall width:	70 in (1.77 m)
Overall height:	70 in (1.77 m)
Ground clearance (min):	7.5 in (190 mm)
Ground clearance under chassis:	12.5 in (318 mm)
Wheelbase:	100 in (2.54 m)
Track:	158.5 in (1.49 m)
Weight: petrol	(Unladen plus 5 gallons fuel) 3800 lb (1724 kg) split 50% on each axle.
Weight: diesel	4408 lb (2000 kg)

Performance	1970 4-speed	1983 5-speed
Top speed:		
Mean (mph)	99.0	96.0
Best (mph)	102.2	98.0
Speed in gears:		
1st	26.0	36.0
2nd	43.0	56.0
3rd	70.0	80.0
4th	99.0	96.0
5th	N/A	95.0
Acceleration from rest (seconds):		
0-30 mph	4.2	3.8
0-40 mph	6.2	6.3
0-50 mph	9.3	9.7
0-60 mph	12.9	14.4
0-70 mph	17.7	20.8
0-80 mph	25.6	32.1
0-90 mph	36.6	49.2
Standing quarter mile (seconds):	18.7	19.5
Acceleration through the gears:		
(seconds) Top gear only.		
20-40 mph	9.1	15.9
30-50 mph	9.1	15.2
40-60 mph	9.4	16.3
50-70 mph	10.6	18.1
Fuel consumption:		
In town:	14.8 mpg	15.4 mpg
Touring:	18.2 mpg	20.1 mpg

NOTE: Fuel injection model.
When announced, it was claimed to have a top speed of 107 mph, and could knock off 2^1/$_2$ seconds from the zero to 60 mph time. Fuel consumption was said to be marginally better, manual version's urban figure being 15.4 mpg and the automatic returning 14.6 mpg.
NOTE: Turbo diesel model.
The makers figures for this model, at launch, were: top speed 90 mph; 0-60 mph in 18.1 seconds; urban fuel consumption 25.5 mpg.

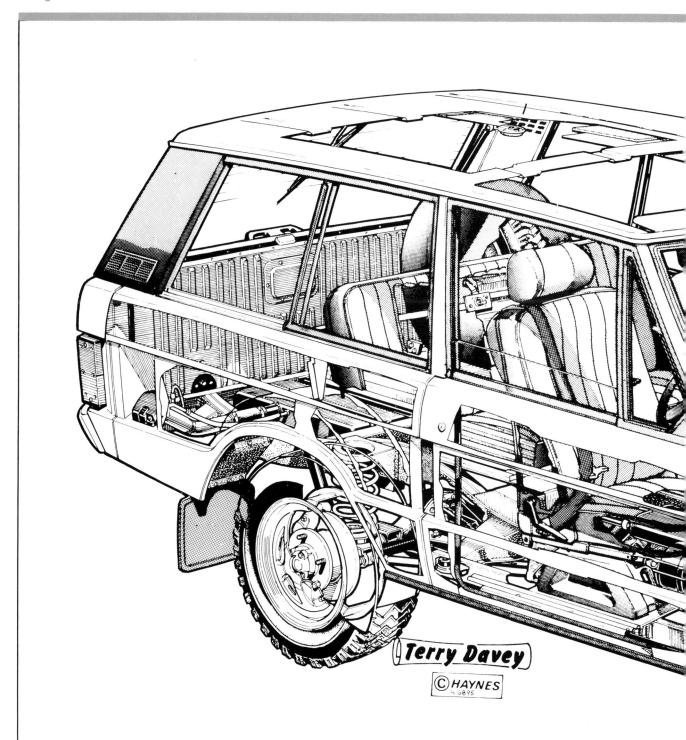

Terry Davey

© HAYNES
H 6895

ROAD TESTS

AUTOTEST
RANGE ROVER
(3,528 c.c.)

AT-A-GLANCE: Vee-8 estate car with constant four-wheel drive and high ground clearance for cross country work. Most impressive ride on or off the road. Cornering very good, but excess roll. Steering rather vague, and heavy at low speeds. Superb driving position and high standard of comfort. Very good brakes and performance.

EAGERLY awaited, the new Range Rover has fulfilled and even surpassed the high hopes held for it. The combination of an over-90 mph maximum speed with the ability to go cross-country mud-plugging as well is not new—the Kaiser Jeep Wagoneer did all this when we tested it in 1964—but will seem revolutionary to many. What is so good about the Range Rover is the way it carries out its multiple functions, serving equally well as tug, load carrier, cross-country vehicle and, by no means least, as an ordinary car suitable even for commuting in heavy traffic.

It is often forgotten how seating positions have been lowered over recent years, to keep waist and roof levels down, and it takes something like the Range Rover, in which one sees over the roof of the car ahead, to make one appreciate the value of a higher sight line. The ability to see what is happening much farther in front, and to be able to look down on the flat bonnet with its clearly defined corners, means it is easier to appraise traffic situations and to place the vehicle accurately. This good view all round goes a long way to compensate for the rather large turning circles and 5ft 10in. width.

Also unexpectedly good is the standard of ride comfort, an education in what can be achieved with live axles front and rear. On most surfaces the car rides with surprisingly little vertical movement, and there is only occasionally a trace of front end pitch—short crisp bounce rather than any suggestion of floating. A big contribution to the ride is

undoubtedly made by the Michelin radial M + S cross-country tyres fitted, which absorb small irregularities and always look a little "squish" when inflated to the recommended 25 psi.

One of the biggest improvements noticed by anyone familiar with the Land-Rover is the very much better ride in cross-country work. Long travel coil springs front and rear, with huge telescopic dampers, absorb rough tracks and field conditions extraordinarily well, and without any of the violent bucking and bouncing of an ordinary leaf spring Land-Rover.

The other respect in which the Range Rover is far superior, of course, is its much greater speed potential. The true level road maximum is 91 mph, at which the speedometer reads 95 mph, while on a downhill straight we obtained an indicated 104 mph. The natural cruising speed is 85 mph, when engine noise is pleasantly restrained and the car feels relaxed and unstressed.

Equally impressive is the acceleration and the Range Rover gives a smart step-off in traffic, which belies its size and makes it often the quickest car away from the lights. Through the gears it accelerates briskly to 80 mph in under half a minute, and the 19.1 sec time for the standing quarter mile is much better than many more lithesome saloons, and only 1.2 sec slower than the Rover 3500. The engine is almost the same all-aluminium vee-8 of 3,528 c.c. as is used in the 3500 and 3.5-litre saloons, but has Zenith-Stromberg CD2 carburettors instead of SUs, and the compression ratio is lowered from 10.5 to 8.5 to 1, suiting it to as low as 91-octane fuel (or 85-octane with reset ignition timing). A pull-out manual enrichment control is provided for cold starting, near the door hinge on the right (rhd model), and can soon be pushed in after a cold start. Throughout the test starting was generally immediate, only once a bit reluctant from cold when standing on a slope. To prevent vapour lock in very hot conditions, particularly with hard work at low speeds, the fuel is recirculated from the right hand carburettor back to the tank.

Not surprisingly, the vee-8 engine seems even smoother in this big car than in the Rover 3500, and its lusty low speed torque enabled us to take acceleration figures in top gear from 10 mph with only mild protest. There are no vibration periods and the noise level is always fairly low. At tickover there is some tremor and slight lumpiness gently rocking the car.

Although the 3500 is only available with automatic transmission, the Range Rover is supplied with four-speed manual gearbox. There is effective synchromesh on all four gears but the gear change itself is very heavy, has rather long travel, and is a bit notchy; at least it goes well with the heavy duty nature of the car. During performance testing it became very difficult to hurry the changes, and in ordinary use a slow, rather deliberate movement, preferably with double-declutching both up and down, helps the gears to go through more easily. The ratios are well spaced, and recommended change points are shown on the speedometer at 26, 43 and 71 mph. Considerably more revs can be used in safety, true maxima for the gears being 30, 49 and 79 mph before the hydraulic tappets begin to pump up. Clutch take-up is smooth, and at 40lb the operating load is not too heavy, even for traffic use. However, towards the end of the test trouble was experienced with the clutch hydraulics, it sometimes tending not to release and at other times being reluctant to engage.

AUTOCAR 12 November 1970

MANUFACTURER
The Rover Company Ltd, Solihull, Warwickshire.

PRICES

Basic	£1,528	12s	7d
Purchase Tax	£469	7s	5d
Seat belts	£7	16s	8d
Total (in G.B.)	£2,005	16s	8d

EXTRAS
None listed

PRICE AS TESTED . . . £2,005 16s 8d

PERFORMANCE SUMMARY

Mean maximum speed	91 mph
Standing start ¼-mile	19.1 sec
0–60 mph	13.9 sec
30–70 mph through gears	14.3 sec
Typical fuel consumption	16 mpg
Miles per tankful	304

AUTOCAR *12 November 1970*

Unlike the Land-Rover and other cross-country vehicles, on which four-wheel drive causes transmission wind-up if used on metalled roads, that on the Range Rover is permanently engaged. Small variations in front-rear wheel revolutions are accommodated by a Salisbury Powr-Lok limited-slip differential installed in the transfer gearbox, and a notice below the facia warns of the special precautions to be taken before testing with only one end of the vehicle on a rolling-road dynamometer.

When alternating between good and bad going, and particularly in snow, it is a great advantage not to have to worry about engaging or disengaging four-wheel drive, and the traction in mud is really remarkable. Just to the right of the gear lever is a small, pull-up knob, by means of which the centre differential can be locked; it works a vacuum-operated pawl, and when engaged a little light comes on in the top of the button as a reminder to free the diff as soon as reasonable grip is regained. Although we gave the Range Rover an extensive work-out over some deeply rutted mud and on one or two almost frighteningly steep gradients, we never had to resort to locking the diff; but again this might be invaluable in conditions of severe snow or ice, or when towing.

As well as the cross-country advantages of permanent four-wheel drive, it pays real dividends in improved cornering. The Range

Far left, top to bottom: The Range Rover's healthy ground clearance enables it to traverse heavily ridged ground without trouble; its high build helps to keep down spray in water-logged conditions and preserve a good view for the driver. Wading (the depth shown is about 18in.) is accomplished with ease, and the Range Rover is quite happy to progress while tilted to one side at a considerable angle Top: The Range Rover is built high, but is compact in plan. With its sensible finish, it looks more at home in these surroundings than it does in town Above: With both halves of the tailgate open, the load platform is of very large area Left: The compact vee-8 engine fits easily beneath the broad, rear-hinged bonnet, with good access to most major components

RANGE ROVER (3,528 c.c.)

AUTOCAR 12 November 1970

ACCELERATION

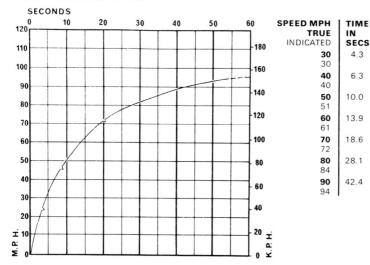

SPEED MPH TRUE INDICATED	TIME IN SECS
30	4.3
30	
40	6.3
40	
50	10.0
51	
60	13.9
61	
70	18.6
72	
80	28.1
84	
90	42.4
94	

SPEED RANGE, GEAR RATIOS AND TIME IN SECONDS

mph	Top (4.16)	3rd (6.25)	2nd (10.17)	1st (16.91)
10-30	10.2	6.2	3.5	3.0
20-40	9.1	5.6	3.8	—
30-50	9.6	6.0	—	—
40-60	9.8	6.6	—	—
50-70	10.6	8.4	—	—
60-80	14.2	—	—	—
70-90	24.4	—	—	—

Standing ¼-mile
19.1 sec 71 mph
Standing Kilometre
35.5 sec 85 mph
Test distance
1,766 miles
Mileage recorder
1 per cent
over-reading

PERFORMANCE
MAXIMUM SPEEDS

Gear	mph	kph	rpm	Low ratio mph	Low ratio kph
Top (mean)	91	146	4,550	42	68
(best)	92	148	4,600	—	
3rd	79	127	5,950	28	45
2nd	49	79	5,970	17	27
1st	30	48	6,100	10	16

BRAKES

(from 70 mph in neutral)
Pedal load for 0.5g stops in lb

1	45	6	45
2	45	7	45
3	45	8	45
4	45	9	45
5	45	10	45

RESPONSE (from 30 mph in neutral)

Load	g	Distance
20lb	0.30	100ft
40lb	0.54	56ft
60lb	0.74	41ft
80lb	0.90	33.4ft
100lb	1.02	29.6ft
Handbrake	0.45	67ft

Max. Gradient on handbrake 1 in 3 (at least)

CLUTCH

Pedal load 40lb and 4in. travel

MOTORWAY CRUISING

Indicated speed at 70 mph	72 mph
Engine (rpm at 70 mph)	3,500 rpm
(mean piston speed)	1,630ft/min.
Fuel (mpg at 70 mph)	16.5 mpg
Passing (50-70 mph)	8.6 sec

COMPARISONS

MAXIMUM SPEED MPH

Volvo 145S estate car	(£1,878)	98
Kaiser Jeep Wagoneer	(not available in UK)	92
Range Rover	**(£1,998)**	**91**
Peugeot 404L Familiale	(£1,499)	87
Land-Rover 6-cyl estate car	(£1,786)	73

0-60 MPH, SEC

Range Rover	**13.9**
Volvo 145S estate car	14.5
Kaiser Jeep Wagoneer	15.5
Peugeot 404L Familiale	19.2
Land-Rover 6-cyl estate car	29.0

STANDING ¼-MILE, SEC

Range Rover	**19.1**
Volvo 145S estate car	19.6
Kaiser Jeep Wagoneer	20.0
Peugeot 404L	21.1
Land-Rover 6-cyl estate car	23.6

OVERALL MPG

Peugeot 404L Familiale	22.2
Volvo 145S estate car	20.7
Kaiser Jeep Wagoneer	14.8
Range Rover	**14.4**
Land-Rover 6-cyl estate car	13.8

GEARING (with 205-16in. tyres)

		Low ratio
Top	20.0 mph per 1,000 rpm	7.1
3rd	13.3 mph per 1,000 rpm	4.7
2nd	8.2 mph per 1,000 rpm	2.9
1st	4.9 mph per 1,000 rpm	1.7

TEST CONDITIONS:
Weather: Cloudy, bright. Wind: 8 mph. Temperature: 16 deg. C. (58 deg. F). Barometer 29.9 in. hg. Humidity: 51 per cent. Surfaces: Dry concrete and asphalt.

WEIGHT:
Kerb weight: 34.7 cwt (3,880lb—1,758kg) (with oil, water and half full fuel tank). Distribution, per cent F, 49.1; R, 50.9. Laden as tested: 38.4 cwt (4,300lb—1,950kg).

TURNING CIRCLES:
Between kerbs L, 37ft 3in.; R, 38ft 6in. Between Walls L, 38ft 10in.; R, 40ft 4in., steering wheel turns, lock to lock 3.7.

Figures taken at 2,500 miles by our own staff at the Motor Industry Research Association proving ground at Nuneaton.

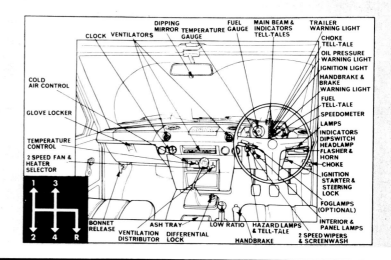

RANGE ROVER (3,528c.c.) *AUTOCAR 12 November 1970*

CONSUMPTION

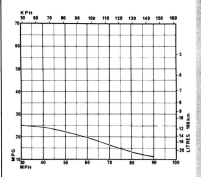

FUEL
(At constant speeds—mpg)

30 mph	25.1
40 mph	24.3
50 mph	22.1
60 mph	19.5
70 mph	16.5
80 mph	13.7
90 mph	11.8

Typical mpg 16 (17.7 litres/100km)
Calculated (DIN) mpg 15.0 (18.8 litres/100km)
Overall mpg . . . 14.4 (19.6 litres/100km)
Grade of fuel . . Regular, 2-star (min. 85 RM)

OIL
Miles per pint (SAE 20W) 300

SPECIFICATION FRONT ENGINE, FOUR-WHEEL DRIVE

ENGINE
Cylinders . . . 8, in 90 deg vee
Main bearings . 5
Cooling system . Water; pump, fan and thermostat; cross-flow radiator
Bore . . . . . 88.9mm (3.5 in.)
Stroke . . . . 71.1mm (2.8 in.)
Displacement . . 3,528 c.c. (215 cu.in.)
Valve gear . . . Overhead, pushrods and hydraulic tappets
Compression ratio 8.5-to-1 Min. octane rating: 85 RM
Carburettors . . Two Zenith Stromberg CD2
Fuel pump . . . AC Delco mechanical
Oil filter . . . Full flow external, disposable
Max. power . . . 135 bhp (net) at 4,750 rpm
Max. torque . . 205 lb.ft (net) at 3,000 rpm

TRANSMISSION
Clutch . . . . Single dry plate, diaphragm spring: 10.5 in. dia.
Gearbox . . . Four-speed, all-synchromesh, centre change

Gear ratios . . .

		Transfer gearbox	
Top 1.0			
Third 1.505		High 1.174	
Second 2.448		Low 3.321	
First 4.069			
Reverse 3.664			

Final drives . . Spiral bevel with enclosed universal joints; (front) 3.54 to 1

CHASSIS and BODY
Construction . . Welded box chassis frame with steel base unit; body panels mainly in aluminium

SUSPENSION
Front . . . . . Live axle on coil springs with radius arms and Panhard rod. Telescopic dampers
Rear . . . . . Live axle on coil springs with radius arms, support rods and central A-bracket. Boge Hydromat self-levelling strut. Telescopic dampers

STEERING
Type . . . . . Burman recirculating ball, worm and nut
Wheel dia. . . . 16¾ in.

BRAKES
Make and type . Lockheed discs all round, twin hydraulic circuits
Servo . . . . . Direct-acting Lockheed vacuum
Dimensions . . F 11.75 in. dia. discs, R 11.42 in. dia. discs

Handbrake . . . 7.25 in. dia. 3 in. wide shoes (on rear of transfer box)
Swept area . . . F 252 sq.in., R 244 sq.in. Total 496 sq.in. (258 sq.in./ton laden)

WHEELS
Type . . . . . Pressed Rostyle enamelled, 5-stud fixing 6 in. wide rim
Tyres—make . . Michelin M + S
  —type . . radial ply tubed
  —size . . 205-16 in.

EQUIPMENT
Battery . . . . 12 Volt 57 Ah negative earth
Alternator . . . Lucas 16ACB 34 amp a.c.
Headlamps . . . 7 in. dia. sealed units 150 watt (total)
Reversing lamp . No provision
Electric fuses . 4
Screen wipers . 2-speed
Screen washer . Standard, electric
Interior heater . Standard, fresh air blending
Heated backlight No provision
Safety belts . . Extra: anchorages built into seat frames
Interior trim . . Pvc seats, Pvc on Fibreglass headlining
Floor covering . Moulded pvc; rubber in load compartment
Jack . . . . . Screw pillar, winding handle
Jacking points . None—use axle casings
Windscreen . . Toughened

MAINTENANCE
Fuel tank . . . 19 Imp. gallons (no reserve) (86 litres)
Cooling system . 20 pints (including heater)
Engine sump . . 10 pints (5.68 litres) SAE 20W. Change oil every 5,000 miles. Change filter element every 5,000 miles.
Gearbox . . . . 4.5 pints SAE 80EP. Change oil every 5,000 miles
Transfer gearbox 5.5 pints Castrol Hypoy LS or equivalent. Change oil every 5,000 miles
Final drives . . 4.5 pints (front), 2.75 pints (rear) SAE 80EP. Change oil every 20,000 miles (or monthly under severe wading conditions)
Grease . . . . one point every 5,000 miles, and one point every 20,000 miles
Tyre pressures . F 25: R 25 psi (normal driving) F 25: R 35 psi (full load)
Max. payload . . 1,500 lb (680 kg)

PERFORMANCE DATA
Top gear mph per 1,000 rpm 20.0
Mean piston speed at max. power . . . 2,220 ft/min
Bhp per ton laden . . . . 70.3 (net)

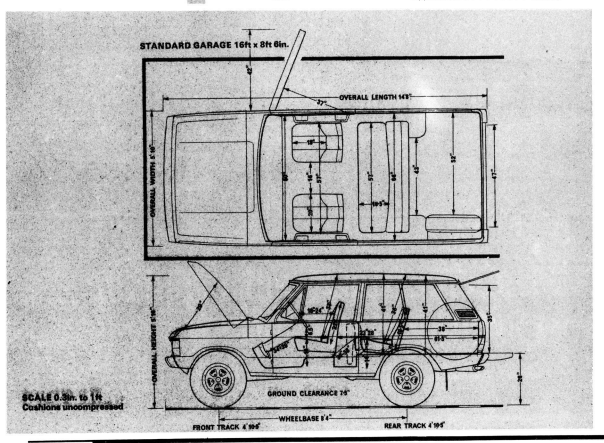

STANDARD GARAGE 16ft x 8ft 6in.

OVERALL LENGTH 14'8"

OVERALL WIDTH 5'10"

OVERALL HEIGHT 5'10"

SCALE 0.3in. to 1ft
Cushions uncompressed

GROUND CLEARANCE 7'9"

FRONT TRACK 4'10⅝"
WHEELBASE 8'4"
REAR TRACK 4'10⅝"

Super Profile

AUTOTEST
RANGE ROVER . . .

Rover behaves as a rather strong understeerer, but when the power is applied hard the front wheels can be felt pulling the car round without any protest from the tyres. On slippery surfaces there is some straight-on effect as the front wheels lose their grip but the car quickly recovers when the throttle is eased back. Rather alarming roll angles can be achieved when cornering hard, and roll stiffness generally could well be improved.

At low speeds the steering effort required becomes very heavy indeed and it is quite a battle to manoeuvre the Range Rover in a confined car park. On the straight at speed there is some play, and it was disappointing to find the directional stability not as good as had been hoped for, especially in side winds. Excellent freedom from kick back in rough cross country work is the best feature of the steering, and an important factor for such a car.

Disc brakes with servo assistance give really dependable braking and progressive increase in efficiency as pedal load goes up, until an impressive 1.02g maximum is achieved at 100lb pedal load. There is little tendency for the wheels to lock under hard braking on slippery roads, and fade testing did not bring any fall-off in efficiency although the front discs became very hot, causing lubricant to dribble out of the front hub on the left. The pedals are well placed, allowing easy heel-and-toe operation, and they are big enough to suit a driver wearing gum boots.

The pull-up handbrake beside the driver's left knee operates a separate drum brake on the rear transmission and—through the limited slip differential—has some effect on the front wheels as well. It holds easily on 1 in 3, and is exceptionally efficient as an emergency brake, giving 0.45g in return for a strong pull.

In our preliminary impressions of the Range Rover at announcement time (18 June), it was mentioned that transmission whine was expected to be reduced in production cars, and it is indeed much better, although still quite noticeable in the middle speed ranges in top gear. The high-pitched whine is difficult to distinguish from tyre hum caused by the coarse tread blocks.

To the right of the main gearbox is the transfer gearbox, with its small stubby change lever and straight dog engagement. Without double-declutching, the vehicle must come to a complete standstill before going into low ratio. Maximum speeds in low are 10, 17, 28 and 42 mph, and the gearing in low ratio first gives less than 2 mph per 1,000 rpm, enabling the Range Rover to climb almost any gradient on which it can find adequate grip. It is difficult to take off smoothly in low ratio bottom gear, and usually second or third can be used for starting when low is engaged.

A small but surprising criticism is that the transfer box lever is a simple rubber push fit on the actuating stub and after moderate normal use it fell off.

The Range Rover body style is standardized as a two-door estate car with sliding rear side windows, swivelling front quarter vents and winding side windows in the doors. The rear window is released by a locking press button, and gas-filled struts automatically push it open. A lever above the number plate is moved sideways to release the bottom hinged tail panel which is located at the horizontal by strong supports, making a sturdy rearward extension of the load platform. Maximum payload is over half a ton with two adults on board as well, and a self-energizing strut in the rear suspension A-bracket quickly pumps itself up within the first few yards, restoring normal ride attitude when laden. Loaded to the limit, it made the rear suspension much harsher, but certainly offset any tail sag.

The seats are excellently shaped, with just the right back support, and are softly sprung with deep foam rubber. Although there is no adjustment, the backrest angle is good, and there is ample fore and aft adjustment. Safety belts are mounted directly on to the seat structure, with incidental advantages that they are not in the way of access to the rear compartment, and that they are more comfortable when worn than when sat on.

Rather awkwardly placed, a lever on the inside of each front seat is raised to free the backrest, which can then be pulled forward for access to the rear compartment. As it moves forward, the seat cushion also slides forward, and it is as easy to get into the back as to the front. Behind the rear seat squab is a central lever which is moved sideways to release the backrest for extra load capacity. In the usual estate car fashion, the squab folds against the cushion, and the whole seat then tips forward against the front seats. A strap is provided to hold the back seat squab tightly against the cushion.

Neat column-mounted levers control the two-speed wipers and the screen washers (press in), head lamp dipping, and optional fog lamps, as well as the usual functions for head lamp flashing and indicators.

Through-flow ventilation is provided, with the unusual provision of a small catch by means of which the extractor vents can be closed off (perhaps for sand storms?). The heater is of air blending type, and responds well to adjustment of the temperature lever. Another lever beneath it controls air input with half and full speed fan positions for both fresh and recirculating air. A vertical lever on the left admits cool air through a centre inlet with adjustable vanes, and the matching lever on the right is for air direction to screen or floor. In addition to the centre ventilator, there are separate ball-in-socket outlets.

Interior stowage

A fairly spacious drop-down locking facia pocket is fitted in front of the passenger, and there is a well for oddments in the top of the facia above it. A facia locker to the right of the steering column appears to be the only possible position for mounting a radio. A large circular speedometer is mounted in a raised nacelle ahead of the driver, includes kilometre markings and a trip mileometer, and is matched by a circular dial in which are temperature and fuel gauges. A clock is standard, on the left of the facia centre, and there are blanks for three more instruments to be added. Between the main instruments are the six warning tell-tales in a vertical arrangement including one for trailer lights.

In our two-week spell with the Range Rover we amassed 1,766 miles, including trips to South Wales and the Lake District. Our overall fuel consumption of 14.4 mpg therefore includes a lot of long runs to offset the heavy consumption of cross-country work. The best intermediate figure was 15.3 mpg, and although this naturally includes high cruising speeds and brisk driving, it would be unrealistic for an owner to expect more than about 17 mpg in general service. On the test car the fuel filler was very stiff and difficult to open. When locked, it freewheels. The tank holds 19 gallons, with the warning tell-tale coming on for the last three.

We have been tremendously impressed by the Range Rover, and feel it is even more deserving of resounding success than the Land-Rover. It remains to be seen how durable and reliable it will prove in service, and to find out we plan to add one to our long-term test fleet as soon as possible.   □

The very large doors give good access to the wide, bench-type back seat, helped by the special release mechanism on the front seats, and belts which do not get in the way

Although devoid of bright trim, the dashboard looks smart and businesslike. There is plenty of evidence of the comprehensive ventilation system, but three of the instrument spaces are blanks

There is plenty of width in the rear for three passengers, and the seat cushion and squab are quite comfortable; but sideways support is lacking and there are no proper elbow rests at the ends

Strong springs retain some parts of the comprehensive tool kit, and elastic straps the rest. They are situated on the same side as the fuel tank filler neck; the 19-gallon tank is beneath the floor

MOTOR week ending January 25 1975

2

BRIEF TEST

RANGE ROVER

FOR : incredible cross-country ability ; fast, comfortable long-distance cruiser ; brilliant blend of the practical and the luxurious ; excellent visibility
AGAINST : thirsty ; noisy gear train ; slow gear change ; non-assisted steering low-geared and heavy at low speed

Unique, ultra-versatile, rugged, practical, luxurious, sophisticated and charismatic are adjectives commonly applied to the Range Rover—and each of them is apt. It is the only vehicle (to call it a car is to ignore its cross-country potential) that is equally at home in Park Lane, the Sahara, the Darien Gap, a cart track or a ploughed field. When it was introduced in 1970 Peter Wilks, then technical director of Rover, said that they " set to work to produce something that had Land-Rover utility, ruggedness and so on, but with more performance and something approaching a car-type refinement and luxury."

Rover not only succeeded, but in doing so produced a vehicle that was a hit from the start, with demand always higher than supply as the second-hand resale value indicated.

Different the Range Rover most certainly is, and impossible to categorise. It is not just a comfortable Land Rover nor a four-wheel-drive saloon: it is both those and a lot more besides. It will cruise comfortably and quietly on a motorway at 90 mph

for as long as you like, yet will climb mountains, slog through axle-deep mud in the lowest of its eight gears, and will traverse roads so bad that driver and passengers are flinching, expecting the worst, at speeds that are almost unbelievable. Most vehicles are a compromise, and the Range Rover is no exception, so there are things to criticise: but seldom, even in more ordinary and dull cars, have so many compromises been worked out so acceptably.

What goes to make the Range Rover so brilliant ? There is a sturdy box-section chassis, for a start: old fashioned but immensely rugged and reliable. On top of this is a steel framework and inner pannelling (much like that of the Rover 2000 saloon) to which the outer panels, most being made of aluminium, are attached. The engine is a low compression ratio version of Rover's all-aluminium V8, producing a fairly modest 130 bhp at only 5000 rpm. More impressive is the 185 lb ft of torque at 2500 rpm which goes a long way to explaining the almost steam-engine like pull at low revs.

Constant four-wheel-drive is a feature of the transmission, via a differential beside the four-speed gearbox to cater for any speed differences between the front and rear axles. As well as the normal four-speed gearbox there is a transfer box with high and low ranges, to give anything from 20.1 mph/1000 rpm in top/high for comfortable motorway cruising down to 1.7 mph/1000 rpm in bottom/low for really sticky conditions. The only overlap that occurs between the eight forward ratios is that top/low is quite close to second/high and third/low is almost identical to first high—some overlap is to be expected. One final piece of icing on the cake for near impossible conditions is a vacuum operated lock on the central diff, for use when either axle starts spinning both wheels at once.

Live axles at both ends also seem old fashioned, but the suspension system of the Range Rover is about as far from the typical pre-war set up as it is possible to be. Solid axles and large wheels give exceptional ground clearance, and that is a prerequisite for any off-road vehicle. The axles are properly located by radius arms and a Panhard rod at the front and radius arms and an A-frame at the rear. Long supple springs, telescopic dampers and a self-energising hydraulic levelling strut acting on the differential soak up the bumps.

Like most aspects of the Range Rover the performance can be considered in a dual light. As a large comfortable 3.5 litre saloon or estate it is nothing special: 15.0 secs from a standing start to 60 mph is mediocre, being comparable to such cars as the Ford Cortina 1600 and the Citroen GS 1220 Club. On the other hand it does hold an indicated 90 mph with ease, is no embarrassment away from traffic lights, will pull from as low as 15 mph in top (but gear snatch prevents such action being used very often) and is almost turbine smooth, refined and quiet at speed—all unexpected attributes of a cross country vehicle. A large engine, 34.3 cwt, a complicated gear train, a huge frontal area and a shape that has

been described as " akin to a slightly rounded brick " do mean, however, that fuel consumption suffers to the extent of about 14 mpg overall, with a best (driven gently in the country) of 15.6 mpg.

Another by-product of a lengthy gear train is inertia, and that partially explains the almost agricultural gearchange, which is baulky, ungainly, and slow. Reverse seldom engages without a graunch, while rushed changes anywhere else caught out the synchromesh. Transmission whine and zizz too is one of the worst offenders when it comes to noise. But then the Range Rover is not a sports car, and considering the complexity of the system, the number of ratios which it makes available and the consequent versatility of the vehicle as a whole the change is quite acceptable —if you take matters slowly it clunks home quite nicely, and you soon get used to it. On MIRA's cross-country track we were taking it through mudholes and across ground that looked impassable : not only did it cope, but we seldom had to resort to the low range, never mind the diff lock. It really would take incredibly deep glutinous mud to bog the RR down, and even then we suspect that it would simply inch its way out in the lowest of the eight gears.

Even more remarkable is the speed at which it can take seemingly impossibly rough farm roads composed of potholes, rocks, bumps, humps and mud : speaking of the MIRA cross-country track the only limit to speed was set by either driver courage or mud splashed so thick and often on the windscreen that the wipers could not cope. There is no violent steering kick back, although a light touch (letting it find its own path) is best. It sails across such surfaces with aplomb and with a ride that is little short of incredible, the long travel springs simply allowing the car to heave and lurch gently and never to bottom on the bump stops.

Some of the ordinary road handling is traded off for this cross country ability, but surprisingly little. The steering is

27

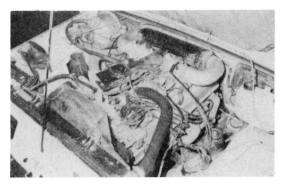

Plenty of space all round the engine makes it easy to work on

low geared (4.75 turns lock to lock), but the optional power steering compensates by requiring only 3.5 turns. Unassisted, it is heavy and ponderous when parking, requires a lot of twirling on tight corners and almost as much untwirling due to the poor self-centring, and is vague about the dead ahead, while the long supple springs and high body do mean a fair bit of roll: but that really is about all the criticism you can level at it. It is stable and reassuring on corners, while the understeer and lift-off tuck-in are not very pronounced.

At £149.35 including tax, the optional power steering completely transforms the Range Rover for town use. As one would expect, the assistance takes all the strain out of parking in confined spaces, and in addition its considerably higher gearing (3.5 turns) means far less work for all in-town motoring. There is still a slight vagueness about the straight-ahead position, but by general standards the system is well weighted and therefore has a fair degree of feel.

The brakes are powerful and progressive, but the handbrake is a bit awkward to reach, and there is a slightly disconcerting lurch forwards or backwards (depending on whether the RR is facing uphill or down) when the handbrake is applied, due to the play in the transmission: the handbrake operates a drum brake on the back of the transfer box.

Height and width rather than length characterise the cavernous interior. The two separate front seats are set far enough apart to fit another (if the transmission tunnel weren't there) and there is a bench at the back that can take three quite happily. The rear door splits horizontally so that the long loads can be carried sticking out the back (the bottom half when open lies flush with the floor), and the rear seat does a double roll forward to increase the load space. The only complaint from rear seat passengers was a lack of support from the rather slippery and flat seat, so that they tend to slide around a little.

Most drivers found the front seats very comfortable, although one or two could have done with more thigh support. The non-inertia belts are fiddly to fit but

Top: a flat floor goes with the huge luggage area. (Above): the transfer box lever is next to the ashtray, the diff lock button at the bottom of the gear lever

are contained within the seat so once set do not require readjusting if the seat is moved —a good thing too, for when the non-adjustable backrest is folded forward to gain access to the rear the whole seat moves and has to be re-set each time: a tiresome chore. The vinyl on the seats of the test car is much more practical, wiping clean instantly.

For those not intent on using their RR specifically for farm use, the less utilitarian nylon seat trim (£19.07 extra) would appear to be a good buy. Not only does it look smarter and grip you better, but it's also softer and generally more comfortable than the standard vinyl variety.

Most of the major controls are within easy reach, only the hand brake causing any bother. Apart from the main gearlever there is a stubby little one behind it for the transfer box, and a small push-pull button for the diff lock within the main gear lever gaiter. The minor controls are hap-

The large, comfortable and practical seats incorporate the belts, while the shin-bin is typically Rover.

A neat and stylish facia, but minor controls could be better located, while the two instruments on the left are invisible to the driver.

There are door handles each end of the armrests.

Super Profile

hazardly spread around with no fewer than four stalks on the column. The two on the left operate the fog lights and the wipers and washers, the two on the right the lights and the indicators and dip/flash.

The two main instruments are contained in a neat binnacle atop the facia, with a vertical row of warning lights between them. In addition to these two (which contain the water temperature and fuel gauges on the left and the speedometer on the right) there is an oil pressure gauge (while not doubting its necessity we do question its positioning, in front of the passenger) a clock, an ammeter and an oil pressure gauge—the latter two hidden by the steering wheel spoke.

There is a particularly comprehensive heating and ventilating system, whose controls take a little time to master (especially in the dark as they are unlit) but once learnt provide a condition for almost all situations. Fresh air for the face can come either from two eyeball vents or two slots, all in the middle of the facia.

Wind noise is well suppressed, with very little more at 90 mph than there is at 50. The engine too seldom intrudes, even at maximum revs as delineated by marks on the speedometer but there is an annoying boom at an indicated 80 mph. The main offenders however, are transmission whine and tyre roar, but these are kept to very acceptable limits, considering the dual personality of the RR.

Utilitarian yet smart and comfortable sums up the finish. The interior is finished in plain shades of brown or black, with rubber mats on all the floors and carpeting only on the transmission tunnel. The blend between opulence and practicality is just about right, so that in the saloon mode it does not feel too agricultural, yet it can cope with muddy boots and other dirt collecting objects with ease. The list of fittings, too, is quite comprehensive, with the aforementioned oil temperature gauge (but no tachometer) a rear window wash/wipe facility plus demister, wing mirrors, a cigar lighter, a hazard warning system, and a dipping rear view mirror as standard—the only optional extras are power steering, a radio, Sundym tinted glass, a laminated windscreen, brushed nylon trim and—not unexpectedly—towing equipment.

A high boxy shape, big glass area, and high seats add up to visibility that is not just good but unrivalled. The panoramic view all round makes placing the car easy, while the ability to see over other cars or hedges and spot potential hazards in plenty of time is useful.

As we said at the beginning, the Range Rover is unique, but not just because of the concept but also because it is a brilliant blend of compromises—it does so many things so well. It isn't perfect, but there are few cars which can even begin to compete. We love it!

MOTOR ROAD TEST No. 3/75 • RANGE ROVER

PERFORMANCE

CONDITIONS

Weather	Dry, sunny, wind 0-8 mph
Temperature	44 F
Barometer	30.3 in Hg
Surface	Tarmac

MAXIMUM SPEEDS

	mph	kph
Banked circuit	95.5	153.7
Best ¼ mile	100.0	160.9
Terminal speeds:		
at ¼ mile	68	109
at kilometer	84	135
at mile	94	151
Speed in gears (at 5200 rpm):		
1st	26	42
2nd	44	71
3rd	70	113

ACCELERATION FROM REST

mph	sec	kph	sec
0-30	4.5	0-40	3.5
0-40	6.7	0-60	6.1
0-50	11.2	0-80	11.0
0-60	15.0	0-100	16.0
0-70	20.2	0-120	24.4
0-80	30.4	0-140	39.7
0-90	45.9		

Stand'g ¼ 19.5 Stand'g km 37.0

ACCELERATION IN TOP

mph	sec	kph	sec
20-40	10.2	40-60	5.1
30-50	10.2	60-80	6.8
40-60	11.1	80-100	7.1
50-70	12.3	100-120	9.2
60-80	15.7		

FUEL CONSUMPTION

Touring*	15.9 mpg 17.7 litres/100 km
Overall	13.9 mpg 20.4 litres/100 km

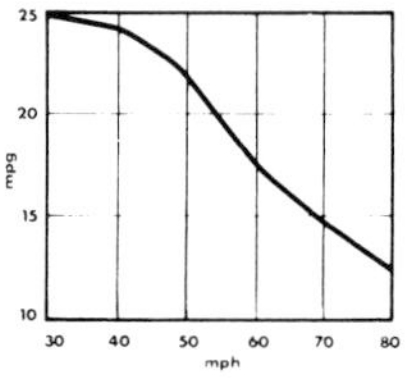

Fuel grade	91 octane (RM) 2 star rating
Tank capacity	19 galls 86 litres
Max range	302miles 487 km
Test distance	1944 miles 3128 km

*Consumption midway between 30 mph and maximum less 5 per cent for acceleration.

SPEEDOMETER (mph)

Speedo	30	40	50	60	70	80	90
True mph	27	36	46	55	64	73	83

Distance recorder: 1 per cent fast

WEIGHT

Unladen weight*	34.3	1742.5
Weight as tested	38.0	1930.5
Weight distribution	50 50	

*with fuel for approx 50 miles

Performance tests carried out by Motor's staff at the Motor Industry Research Association proving ground, Lindley.

GENERAL SPECIFICATION

ENGINE

Cylinders	V8
Capacity	3528 cc (215 cu in.)
Bore/stroke	88.9/71.1 mm (3.5/2.8 in.)
Cooling	Water
Block	Aluminium alloy LM25
Head	Aluminium alloy LM25
Valves	Ohv
Valve timing	
inlet opens	30° btdc
inlet closes	75° abdc
ex opens	68° bbdc
ex closes	37 atdc
Compression	8.25 : 1
Carburetter	2 Zenith Stromberg CD25
Bearings	5 main
Fuel pump	Electrical
Max power	130 bhp (DIN) at 5000 rpm
Max torque	185 lb ft (DIN) at 2500 rpm

TRANSMISSION

Type	4-speed manual with high and low ranges
Clutch	10.5 in. Sdp diaphragm spring

Internal ratios and mph/1000 rpm (high range)

Top	1.00 : 1/20.1
3rd	1.505 : 1/13.4
2nd	2.448 : 1/8.2
1st	4.069 : 1/4.9
Rev	3.664 : 1
Final drive	3.54 : 1
Transfer box	(high range) 1.174 : 1 (low range) 3.321 : 1

BODY/CHASSIS

Construction	Box section chassis with steel framed body shell. Aluminium outer panels
Protection	Heavy gauge steel, stove enamelled. Phosphated steel inner body panels.

SUSPENSION

Front	Live axle, coil springs, radius arms and Panhard rod
Rear	Live axle, coil springs, radius arms and A-frame. Self-levelling central strut

STEERING

Type	Burman recirculating ball
Assistance	Optional
Toe-out	1.8 0.6 mm
Camber	0
Castor	3
King pin	7

BRAKES

Type	Discs all round
Servo	Yes
Circuit	Twin
Rear valve	Yes
Adjustment	Self-adjusting

WHEELS

Type	Pressed steel, 6.0 JK x 16
Tyres	Michelin XM+S radials, 205 x 16
Pressures	25 F, 25 R (35 R laden)

ELECTRICAL

Battery	12V 60 Ah
Polarity	Negative
Generator	Alternator
Fuses	3
Headlights	75 50 W 7 in. sealed beam

COMPARISONS

	Capacity cc	Price £	Max mph	0-60 sec	30-50* sec	Overall mpg	Touring mpg	Length ft in	Width ft in	Weight cwt	Boot cu ft
Range Rover	3528	3924	95.5	15.0	10.2	13.9	15.9	14 8	5 10	34.3	—
BMW 525	4024	2494	114.1	10.2	9.7	20.5	24.7	15 2	5 7	26.3	13.0
Citroen DS23 Safari	2347	2900	104.4	11.3	14.0	20.4	—	16 6	5 11	27.7	—
Ford Granada Estate	2994	3218	105.1	12.2	4.4	16.8	20.8	15 5	5 11	28.6	—
Mercedes 230/4	2307	3825	101.6	12.3	10.8	21.8	23.0	15 4	5 10	26.1	13.5
Peugeot 504 Estate	1971	2491	96.7	13.7	10.3	23.6	24.6	15 9	5 6.5	25.6	—
Reliant Scimitar GTE	2994	3337	123.0	8.7	7.6	21.7	28.2	14 2.25	5 5	22.8	—
Triumph 2.5 PI Estate†	2498	2710	110.5	9.7	8.6	22.2	—	14 6.75	5 5.5	23.9	—
Toyota Crown 2600 Est.	2563	2724	98.1	12.2	4.8	19.6	21.1	15 4.5	5 6.5	27.5	—

*in top/kickdown †figures for equivalent saloon

Make: Rover

Model: Range Rover

Maker: Rover-Triumph British Leyland (UK) Ltd, PO Box 2, Lode Lane, Solihull, Warwicks.

Price: £3354.00 basic plus £279.50 car tax plus £290.68 VAT equals £3924.18

Autocar, w/e 24 December 1983

Range Rover 4-dr 5-speed AutoTEST UPDATE

£15,374 ☐ Max: 96 mph ☐ 0-60 mph: 14.4 sec ☐ 15.4 mpg overall

Range Rover may roll a lot, but it corners remarkably well at speeds most owners wouldn't believe

ROBUST VERSION of well-tried Rover 5-speed gearbox gives Range Rover quieter, fuss-free high-speed cruising capability and – theoretically – better fuel consumption. Used with the new Land Rover LT 230 R transfer box, the new transmission has reduced lever travel, a more positive feel and there is much less transmission "shunt".

MODEL TESTED: Five-speed, four-door, 3.5-litre V8-cyl ohv engine 125 bhp (PS-DIN).

FOR:
- *Fuss-free cruising ability*
- *Excellent off-road capability*

AGAINST:
- *Poor fuel economy*

THE MANUAL transmission has always been the least refined aspect of the Range Rover. It had to be a rugged gearbox to cope with the high torque loads in sustained low ratio work in arduous off-road conditions, so the well-tried Land Rover unit with its incorporated transfer box was the obvious – if rather agricultural – choice.

Hence the luxurious Range Rover, with its so-refined all-alloy V8 engine and super-compliant suspension inherited this long, spindly gear shift lever and distinctly Vintage change quality, clunky and requiring long, deliberate movements. There was also quite a lot of driveline "shunt" and quite obtrusive gear whine.

This has now changed. The gearbox is an adapted version of the 77mm Rover unit, strengthened and with altered ratios, driving through the recently-developed separate LT 230 R transfer box. Together these more modern, mechanically

more refined gearboxes give the Range Rover the smoother, quieter transmission it has always deserved.

The gear shift lever is shorter, has reduced throw and has a much more positive change quality, so the Range Rover is immediately more car-like to drive.

As part of their continuing programme of general improvements, Land Rover have added central door locking, a useful central console and a counterbalance system on the tailgate as standard equipment on the Range Rover, which is now available in either two- or four-door form and with either the five-speed manual of three-speed automatic (Chrysler Torqueflite) transmissions.

Improved mechanical refinement is not the only advantage of the five-speed gearbox. Better spacing of the ratios means improved mid-range performance and the higher, overdrive, top should give better fuel economy. The better performance was im-

mediately noticeable, but the improvement in economy was more elusive.

Land Rover Ltd. claim 10 per cent better consumption, but our overall test figure of 15.4 mpg is worse than the 16.2 mpg we recorded from the four-speed model we tested in October 1981.

The overall figure could be misleading, since we did subject the five-speed to a lot of low-ratio, off-road work during which consumption dropped to 8.4 mpg. On the road, however, the best interim figure we recorded was 17.6 mpg, which is still not 10 per cent better than the average

Shorter, leather-gaitered gearchange lever is clearly marked; its action is more precise, more car-like than the spindly four-speed change lever. Stubby second lever is for range-change and differential lock

Autocar, w/e 24 December 1983

Luxury limousine or workhorse? Fold the rear seat, drop the tailgate and Range Rover offers a big, flat-floored load space. Rear carpeting is part of luxury option pack

recorded with the four-speed. It cannot be denied that the potential for fuel saving is there if good use is made of the overdrive top gear; it is also obvious that economy does not suffer much in return for the striking improvement in performance.

Top speed of the five-speed is very similar to that of the four-speed — a maintainable mean maximum of 96 mph (95 mph for the four-speed) — but mid-range acceleration is much better. Getting from 30 mph to 50 mph takes 9.9 sec in fourth (13.6sec in the four-speed) and 6.8 sec in third (7.9 sec); the 50-70 mph time in fourth is nearly 4 sec faster.

In pitching second, third and fourth gears lower than in the four-speed box, Land Rover have deprived the Range Rover of an "ideal" top gear. The maximum speed of 96 mph comes up at 4,800 rpm in fourth, 800 rpm over

the peak power speed. Shifting into fifth has top speed wasting away slightly to 95 mph, at 3,600 rpm, 400 rpm below the power peak. The intention obviously is for the lower gearing to give the better mid-range performance rather than pitch fourth a little higher in the hope of improving a top speed which is already considerably over the maximum

permitted limit in this country.

At the same time fifth becomes a near-perfect cruising gear, since 70 mph comes up at 2,700 rpm, only 200 rpm over the peak torque speed.

The Range Rover is a big, tall, cumbersome-looking car, but it is not a heavy beast to drive thanks to the pleasingly weighted power-assisted steering. Parking manoeuvres require little more than fingertip pressure, but assistance reduces with speed so that a firm hand is needed in fast cornering.

The recirculating ball steering lacks feel and is a little vague around the straight-ahead position, which calls for some care when threading through traffic on narrower country roads. The lack of feel is built in on purpose, to isolate the driver from the sort of shocks and kick-back that could be transmitted through the steering when the car is driven over rutted or rocky terrain.

That lack of feel does not prevent the Range Rover from being placed and held accurately in corners. One of the car's rear *impressive features* is its roadholding — straight line stability is excellent, and the car can be thrown into corners much faster than drivers new to the Range Rover would believe possible.

There is a lot of cornering roll, which can be unnerving to the inexperienced. The roll is again a by-product of the car's off-road *alter ego* — it has long-travel suspension unencumbered by anti-roll bars allowing it to cover tortuous terrain with ease. However, the roll does not impair the car's cornering ability. The body may tilt until suspension movement is taken up, but the live axles stay parallel to the road to ensure thoroughly predictable handling. Having said that, cornering *in extremis* can have an inside front wheel lifting, as our illustration shows, but even in this situation the driver is aware only of quite manageable levels of understeer. In less extreme cornering the combination of permanent four-wheel drive and near 50-50 weight distribution results in pleasantly neutral handling.

Reduced levels of gear whine now make the Range Rover a very comfortable long-distance cruiser indeed, since other sources of noise are well subdued. The lack of wind noise is particularly impressive considering the car's bulky shape; there is some hiss and roar from

around the A-posts, but this does not become obtrusive until well above 70 mph. It is only to be expected that the big, coarse-treaded M+S tyres will generate some road noise, but again this does not become obtrusive until quite high cruising speeds are reached. With fifth gear engaged at 70 mph on the motorway it is possible to chat to rear seat passengers without raising the voice.

Inside the Range Rover retains its unexpected levels of elegance, with cloth upholstery and roof lining and fully carpeted floor — including the luggage compartment. Even the spare wheel, mounted upright in the rear compartment, is carpet-covered. The hydraulic bottle jack and a comprehensive tool kit are also stowed under carpeted panel covers.

Instrumentation remains the same — comprehensive as befits a vehicle which could be called into service as an off-road workhorse — including the odd siting of the clock and oil pressure gauge in the heater console, low and on the passenger side. Interestingly, with all its luxury, the Range Rover still does not have recline adjustment for the front seats; perhaps it does not need it, since the seats proved comfortable and supportive enough, and there is plenty of head and legroom for six-footers with the seats as they are.

Our test car had most of the available extras, such as air conditioning, rear seat belts, alloy wheels and metallic paint. Three option packs are offered: Pack C adds front and rear armrests, rear head restraints, wood door cappings and loadspace carpets for a total of £367.52. Pack B adds the alloy wheels and metallic paints for £996.67, and Pack A throws in the air conditioning bringing the total added to £1,899.90.

Taking advantage of the option pack can save money. In our price list accompanying this report the options are individually priced, putting the overall cost of the car up to £18,200. However, add the Option Pack A price to the basic and you get a very well equipped Range Rover for £17,273. □

Performance

RANGE ROVER 5-SPEED

MAXIMUM SPEEDS

Gear	mph	kph	rpm
OD Top (mean)	95	153	3,600
(best)	96	155	3,700
4th (mean)	96	155	4,800
(best)	98	158	4,900
3rd	80	129	5,600
2nd	56	90	6,000
1st	36	58	6,000

ACCELERATION

FROM REST	True mph	Time (sec)	Speedo mph
	30	3.8	30
	40	6.3	41
	50	9.7	51
	60	14.4	63
	70	20.8	75
	80	32.1	87
	90	49.2	99

Standing ¼-mile: 19.5sec, 68 mph
Standing km: 37.1sec, 84 mph

IN EACH GEAR	mph	Top	4th	3rd	2nd
	10-30	—	11.5	6.9	4.4
	20-40	15.9	9.7	6.6	2.2
	30-50	15.2	9.9	6.8	3.5
	40-60	16.3	10.5	7.8	
	50-70	18.1	11.7	10.3	
	60-80	—	15.5	18.4	
	70-90	—	25.7	—	

FUEL CONSUMPTION

Overall mpg: 15.4 (18.3 litres/100km) 3.4 mpl
  Autocar formula: Hard 13.9 mpg
    Driving and Average 16.9 mpg
    conditions Gentle 20.1 mpg

Grade of fuel: Premium, 4-star (98 RM)
Fuel tank: 18 Imp. galls (82 litres)
Mileage recorder reads: 0.4 per cent short

OIL CONSUMPTION

(SAE 15W/40) negligible

WEIGHT

Kerb, 37.9cwt/4,249lb/1,927kg
(Distribution F/R, 50.2/49.8)
Test, 41.5cwt/4,650lb/2,109kg
Max. payload, 1,286lb/583kg

TEST CONDITIONS:

Wind: 11 mph
Temperature: 6.9deg C (43deg F)
Barometer: 29.2in. Hg (991 mbar)
Humidity: 83 per cent
Surface: damp asphalt and concrete
Test distance: 1,042 miles

Figures taken at 11,164 miles by our own staff. All Autocar test results are subject to world copyright and may not be reproduced in whole or part without the Editor's written permission.

SPECIFICATION

ENGINE
Longways four-wheel drive.
Head/block Al. alloy/alloy. 8 cylinders in 90 deg V, dry liners, 5 main bearings.
Water cooled, viscous fan.
Bore, 88.9mm (3.5in.), stroke 71.1mm (2.8in.), capacity 3,528 c.c. (215 cu. in.).
Valve gear ohv, hydraulic tappets, chain camshaft drive. Compression ratio 9.35 to 1. Contact breaker ignition, 2 Zenith-Stromberg 175 CD-SE carburettors.
Max power 125 bhp (PS-DIN) (93.2kW ISO) at 4,000 rpm. Max torque 190 lb.ft. at 2,500 rpm.

TRANSMISSION
Five-speed manual. Single dry plate clutch 10.5in. dia.

Gear	Ratio	mph/1,000 rpm
Top	0.77	25.8
4th	1.00	19.8
3rd	1.4	14.2
2nd	2.13	9.3
1st	3.32	6.0

Final drive gear Hypoid bevels, ratio 3.54.
Transfer box: high 1.192
            low 3.32

SUSPENSION
Front, Live axle, radius arms, Panhard rod, coil springs, telescopic dampers.
Rear, Live axle, radius arms, Panhard rod, coil springs, telescopic dampers plus self-levelling strut.

STEERING
Recirculating ball, power assistance.
Steering wheel diameter 17in., 3.5 turns lock to lock.

BRAKES
Dual, separate circuits. Front 11.8in. (300mm) dia discs. Rear 11.4in. (290mm) dia discs. Vacuum servo. Handbrake, centre lever acting on transmission.

WHEELS
Al. alloy (steel standard), 6in. rims.
Michelin XM+S tyres, size 205R-16 radial, pressures F25 R25 psi (normal driving).

DIMENSIONS
Wheelbase 100.0in. (2,540mm); track, front 58.5in. (1,490mm), rear 58.5in. (1,490mm). Overall length 176.0in. (4,470mm) width 70.0in. (1,780mm), height 71.0in. (1,800mm), ground clearance 7.5in. (190mm). Turning circle 37ft 10in. (11.5m). Boot capacity 36.18/70.8 cu. ft.

What it costs

PRICES

Basic	£12,340.00
Special Car Tax	£1,028.33
VAT	£2,005.25
Total (in GB)	**£15,373.58**
Licence	£85.00
Delivery charge (London)	None
Number plates	£15.00
Total on the Road (exc. insurance)	**£15,473.58**

EXTRAS (inc. VAT)

Automatic transmission	£1,031.55
*Alloy wheels	£386.84
*Rear seat belts	£75.94
*Air conditioning	£1,159.07
*Metallic paint	£1,146.18
*Front mud flaps	£58.75
Tow bar	£94.57
*Fitted to test car	

TOTAL AS TESTED ON THE ROAD	**£18,200.36**

Insurance Group 6

Ex-press vehicle NXC 240H (chassis no. 35500035A) stands in almost the same spot as NXL 235H did fifteen years earlier, right, *posing for the second earliest pamphlet cover. This vehicle is still in regular use. (Author)*

Below. *The same vehicle climbing the steep sides of Blue Hills Mines, Cornwall. The vehicle takes such terrain in its stride. (Author)*

Above. *Another of the earliest vehicles, owned by a Range Rover Register member. This vehicle has covered over 350,000 miles in its sixteen-year life. Both YBV 174H and YBV 175H were left-hand drive.*

Right. *This is another pre-production vehicle; chassis number 35500020A. It is owned by Brian Bashall of Dunsfold Land Rovers, and is still in daily use.*

Pre-production cars had a smooth-finish dashboard moulding. This was, of course, replaced by a 'crocodile skin' finish on production models. This is YVB 172H once again. (Author)

Pictured at Syon Park, London, home of the BL Heritage Museum, VGG 113K poses in the sun. This car was owned by the author for three years, extensively modified and resprayed Vogue Blue. (Author)

(Inset) *Bahama Gold was one of the original six colours and was the first to be discontinued, in 1979. This vehicle belongs to Dave Hulbert who is interviewed in the 'Owners View' section of the book.*

The current owner of this vehicle finished in Bahama Gold, was fortunate when he bought the vehicle in April 1984 with only 32,000 miles on the clock. It remains remarkably original.

(Inset) *A smart addition to Barry Martin's vehicle are the two chrome V8 badges on the upper rear quarter-panels. These were never offered on production cars.*

Artic White replaced Davos White in 1974 although they are virtually identical to the eye. Despite being dominated somewhat by the four-door body, the two-door is still being sold today.

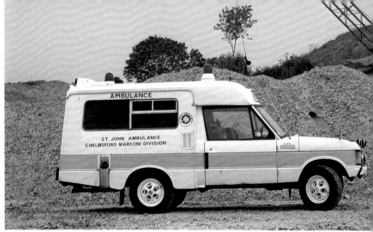

Above left. *A very practical ambulance conversion by Wadham Stringer. Despite being able to speed across rough country, ambulance variants are often criticised as they roll too much – not the best thing for the patient!*

Above. *Most of the rear bodywork is glass fibre on the ambulance conversion, to reduce weight. A 90mph-plus top speed is obtainable, but the cost can be a fuel consumption of only 8 or 10mpg!*

Left. *Carmichael build a superb 6 x 4 fire tender conversion. Indeed, one of the first Range Rovers built – YVB 152H, chassis number 3550002A – was converted in 1971. The vehicle is popular for use at both airports and large factories and has a 200 gallon water tank. (John West)*

Below left. *This conversion is now owned by Martin Han de Beaux and is used for carrying goods and towing. The fire-fighting equipment has been removed from the rear. It does about 10mpg! (John West)*

Bill King, overseas liason officer for the National Association of Rover Clubs, owns this early Vogue. The vehicle was built just a few months before the introduction of the four-door Range Rover.

According to Land Rover Ltd, about 250 Vogues were built for the UK market. It was the first official 'up market' Range Rover and had its own unique picnic hamper in the boot.

David Bowyer, a well known face amongst off-road enthusiasts, arrives at the top of the extremely steep Blue Hills Mine in Cornwall, during the Range Rover 15th birthday celebrations in June 1985, organized by the Range Rover Register.

The engine compartment of an early 1985 Vogue (pre-fuel-injection). Note the large air-conditioning unit at the front.

Above. *Caspian Blue was a very popular colour in 1985, the year of its introduction. Here, a Vogue model poses in one of its natural surroundings.*

Above left. *Pete Hutchings' Artic White 1974 stands behind a Vogue model, some 11 years its junior.*

Left. *A pre-production model, YVB 175H, stands behind the 1985 Caspian Blue Vogue once again. The differences are too numerous to mention, but the overall shape has remained unaltered in the 15$\frac{1}{2}$ years that separate the two cars.*

OWNER'S VIEW

In this section I spoke to Pete Hutchings, who owns a smart Davos White early series 2 Range Rover. Pete is a self-employed chippy and lives in Chelmsford, Essex. Photographs of his vehicle (SXC 237M) are featured in this book.

TA: What was your first car Pete?

PH: I had an old van first of all but my first car was a 1966 Ford Zephyr. I had the Zephyr right up until I bought the Range Rover. First of all though, I had a fair few motorcycles.

TA: How did you first get involved in Range Rovers?

PH: Well, I saw my first one in Springfield Road, Chelmsford. Then I was working in Chingford and I saw one for sale. Not knowing anything about secondhand prices at that time, I thought it might be about £1,500 but on enquiring the price, I found it was going for a lot more than that! I suppose it went on from there.

TA: How long have you had SXC 237M?

PH: I bought it on 17 February 1984.

TA: And what sort of condition was it in when you first bought it?

PH: Well it was not immaculate by a long way. It was generally tidy I suppose. Fair to good really. It had had a respray in its time.

TA: Do you know any of the car's history?

PH: No I don't, but I understand it may have been some sort of company car for a while. I don't know what sort of company would want to run an elderly Range Rover though, do you?

TA: Unless it was for a status symbol?

PH: Yes, but you would think they would have had a newer one.

TA: When you decided to buy a Range Rover, did you go round and look at many?

PH: Oh yes! I hate to think how many I looked at. I suppose it must have been ten or so.

TA: Is it the only vehicle that you have?

PH: Yes it is the only car that I own, but I occasionally use a Reliant three-wheeler van for work. That uses much less fuel!

TA: Do you use it every day including work, or is it a 'weekend car'?

PH: I use it for work a lot but I suppose really I like to think of it as being a weekend car. I hate to spend half a day cleaning it all up only to use it the next day for work and get it thoroughly filthy for no reason at all. I like to come home from work and find it still gleaming parked in a warm dry garage.

TA: Are spare parts cheap and easily available considering its age?

PH: They are not what you call cheap. However parts are easy to get with the car still in production. When I had the Zephyr, I always managed to purchase secondhand parts which were of course cheaper. With the Range Rover, you have to buy them new as there are virtually no vehicles being broken for spares. I suppose if I had bought parts new for the Zephyr, they would have cost almost as much.

TA: Do you consider used Range Rovers to be good value for money?

PH: Yes I think so. They do last longer than the average car what

with their large strong chassis etc. The engine and gearbox are lasting parts, too. Compared to other vehicles they are dear but when you compare – there is no comparison!

TA: A lot of people have had Land Rovers in the past and then gone on to owning Range Rovers. Have you ever considered buying a Land Rover?

PH: No, never.

TA: Why not?

PH: Well its just the general shape of the Range Rover that I like. The Land Rover has never attracted me to it for that reason. Land Rovers can use up a lot more petrol and be very noisy. They have not got the comfort of a Range Rover.

TA: Do you intend keeping it for a long time?

PH: Oh, yes!

TA: How long?

PH: I've no idea really, but if the novelty wears off or I can't afford to run it. That is when it will have to go.

TA: How do you find insurance – is it very dear?

PH: Not really. The older models are of a lower insurance group. It went up this year though to £114 fully comprehensive. It's not too bad. I think mine's group 4 or 5.

TA: Do you put in a lot of effort in keeping it looking nice?

PH: Yes, a fair bit to say the least. It's cleaned when necessary – obviously more in the winter months. I have only really polished it once though, the paint is pretty good so it hasn't really needed any more. The car is garaged anyway so the weather does not get to it too much.

TA: Do you drive it very fast? I sometimes did with mine!

PH: I drive it slowly for economic reasons!

TA: Do you take it off the road at all?

PH: Well I drive off the road just a little. Maybe on the local common but nothing serious.

TA: What sort of fuel consumption have you obtained. I ask that because mine used to do about 15 mpg and up to 18 mpg on a *very* gentle run!

PH: It normally does around 18 mpg but that is, like you said, with gentle driving. I was getting 18 mpg whilst cruising at motorway speeds on the way to the Isle of Man last summer so it is not too bad. I have just fitted a petrol filter kit this week and hope to record a difference.

TA: Is it a reliable car?

PH: Well, it hasn't let me down yet! Sometimes the indicator warning lights do not work, a bad connection somewhere. When I first got it the brakes were not too hot, but on inspection somebody had put parts of the master cylinder in back to front. The brakes are perfect now. Other than that apart from minor problems, it has been fine.

TA: Have you taken any action about fighting any possible rust, and indeed – is there any?

PH: Yes, there is some rust but the chassis is perfect. The rust is just around the sills and up the sides of the front footwells. Oh – and the insides of the bottom rear quarter-panels – around by the back lights. I spray the under-side of the vehicle regularly with oil, well about once every six months. That is something I used to do with the Zephyr and I suppose that is why that lasted so long. Incidentally – the tailgate is fine, but you told me it was not original!

TA: And what modifications would you make if money were no problem?

PH: I wouldn't change the shape at all. I think I would do something to stop the rust. I'd like four doors, but I wouldn't convert mine – it would take too long. No, I'd keep it as it is.

Dave Hulbert owns the remarkably standard Bahama Gold vehicle (HMC 743N) featured in the photo section of this book.

TA: Why are you so interested in the Range Rover?

DH: It is a purely functional vehicle for caravanning, fishing trips, school rugby clubs and putting the bikes in the back syndrome.

TA: When did you buy your Range Rover?

DH: April 1984.

TA: And why?

DH: I required a vehicle with good towing ability for caravanning. A friend in the office had a Range Rover for sale – it had been very well looked after, had a very low mileage for the year, it seemed too good to miss. The fuel consumption was not too important as I have a Mini for everyday use.

TA: What condition was it in when you bought it?

DH: Only one word to describe it, 'superb', with only 32,000 miles on the clock for a nine year old vehicle, it was not surprising.

TA: What are the common problems?

DH: The tailgate has needed a little attention to small scratches in the paintwork and also to some slight rusting. It has had more punctures than any other vehicle I have owned.

TA: What repair or renovation have you done?

DH: Because of the general condition of the bodywork, very little renovation has been required; with a very low mileage, repairs have been minimal.

TA: Have you experienced difficulty in obtaining any parts?

DH: Main problems experienced have been in getting the correct parts for my car due to the inexperience of staff at my local agents. I often have to return parts because they have made mistakes when ordering from the main warehouse.

TA: What kind of performance and handling does the car have?

DH: The overall performance is good, but the gearbox could be better. The steering is good but the vehicle rolls on cornering. I find the transmission noise level quite acceptable.

TA: Is the car in regular and everyday use?

DH: The Range Rover is used irregularly, so the running costs are therefore acceptable.

TA: How would you sum up the enjoyment you get from your Range Rover?

DH: The confidence it gives me when towing is most beneficial. Recently on holiday in the French Alps, towing my caravan, I found the Range Rover handled superbly. The elevated driving position is good when travelling in open country and the big front seats are comfortable on long journeys. The spacious boot is of great use for doing the small jobs that require that extra bit of room, in fact it is a very versatile vehicle.

TA: What advice would you give to potential owners of the Range Rover?

DH: To get one as soon as possible!

BUYING

Historical Value Patterns

It was not long after the launch of the Range Rover that the vehicle's 'one-upmanship' snob value was realised, and this coupled with a short supply of new vehicles for several years put late model second hand prices well over the price of a new vehicle. A black market grew and models were often re-imported. By the end of the seventies, production had finally met the demand in the UK and prices had levelled out, on all but the still-dear early models. More often than not, having a Range Rover was described as 'like having money in the bank'.

Perhaps due to the ever increasing price of petrol, the increased opposition and plentiful supply of both new and late model secondhand vehicles available, by the early eighties second hand prices were very much lower than before. If the trend continues they should drop further still, making the Range Rover a much more affordable car for many more people.

Problem Areas – Mechanical

If a Range Rover has been looked after and regularly serviced, there should not be too much wrong with it. However, the problems start to begin if the vehicle has been subjected to severe off-road use or it has a bad service history. First, let us look at the engine!

The Range Rover engine is a slightly detuned version of the normal Rover V8 found in Rover saloon cars. Examples have been known to last as long as 200,000 miles, before major mechanical overhaul is necessary. However, alarming tales of vehicles covering only 40 or 50 thousand miles and suffering from major problems are not too uncommon. Any engine with tappet noise should be avoided since repair is expensive. (The tappets are self-adjusting and should normally emit no sound). Similarly, exhausts emitting blue smoke indicate worn rings, and steam from the exhaust shows a blown head or inlet manifold gasket. A requirement for constant topping up of the radiator, and no sign of leakage, is also a sure sign of this. Basically though, the engine is a well proven and reliable unit capable of high mileages. Its very long production span goes a long way to prove its makers' confidence in it. The best way to make it last longer is to maintain a regular check on the level of oil and not to forget the routine servicing.

Range Rover gearboxes are tough and durable, but still need looking after. Once again, a regular check on the oil levels is essential. A not uncommon problem is that of constant jumping out of gears. From personal experience, it was found to be nothing more serious than worn detent springs that are accessible from the top of the gearbox with it still in situ. (The springs are very cheap and easy to fit). Noisy gearboxes are common. Noise can be caused simply by a lack of oil or, more seriously, worn bearings. However, gearboxes can operate efficiently for a long time even in this condition rendering expensive replacement unnecessary. Note here that the transfer gearbox has a separate oil reservoir.

Many problems are encountered with the differential lock, which is housed on the back of the gearbox. Locks have been known not to work, or when they do, to stick on. Checks should be made to see if the vacuum pipes have been disconnected or cracked, as a section of pipe is cheaper than a new differential lock unit.

Handbrakes on the earliest models (1970-1972) need constant adjustment. All this needs is someone capable of crawling under the car with a suitable screwdriver every few weeks to keep a constant check. The brake shoes are not expensive, but should not really need replacing very often since the handbrake must not be used as a service brake under any circumstances.

The rear disc brake pads wear very quickly indeed and should be inspected regularly. If they get too low, there is the danger that the pistons will seize up and not return when new pads are fitted. Although piston kits are available, this is not a desirable situation.

Sagging coil springs are common, and vehicles are often known to lean particularly on the driver's side. Unfortunately the springs should be replaced in pairs, (front and rear) but replacement is reasonably easy if spring compressors are on hand. Sagging springs can be the result of overloading.

Vehicles with leaking radiators should be treated with caution as new radiators are expensive, and secondhand units hard to come by. When was the last time you saw a Range Rover on a scrap heap? The Range Rover radiator is not interchangeable with any other vehicle and it would be unsatisfactory to fit a smaller unit from another car.

One final point is that of oil temperature. Early vehicles suffered calibration problems on the oil temperature gauge, so don't be too put off by what seems a high reading!

Problem Areas – Body & Interior

When looking at a secondhand Range Rover, there are numerous items to inspect carefully. Certainly, space does not permit us here to go into too much detail, but the list below lays out some of the major items to pay particular attention to:

Tyres. Are they dual purpose radials? Cross-plies are not suitable.
Lower tailgate. This can rust very quickly.
Upper tailgate frame. This can rust from 'inside out'!
Windows. Do they all wind down or slide properly? Door frames can distort easily.
Panel dents. Look for dents in the soft aluminium panels.
Trim panels. Look for signs of ripping and warping from heat.
Self levelling strut. Does it still function properly? New units are expensive.
Seating. Are covers fitted? Look underneath to see why.

Chassis. It is unlikely that it has rotted through, but vehicles used for towing boats may have been subjected to salt water and this can get into the chassis and start corrosion, particularly in the rear cross-member.

New parts, albeit expensive, are not difficult to obtain as the vehicle is still in production, and is sure to be for many years to come. Total rebuilds are often performed on elderly 'tired' examples. The fact that the Range Rover is not of the modern unitary construction but makes use of a separate chassis to which the components are bolted, makes a total rebuild project much more attractive.

Best Models – But Where?

Because a Range Rover always retains a relatively high value for its age, the average first time Range Rover buyer will probably aim for a vehicle on the older end of the scale. For this reason, it can sometimes be difficult to gain access to a particular vehicles's history. Obviously, the best deal in a second-hand model would be a genuine one owner, garage-serviced-from-new-vehicle, but such opportunities occur rarely. Even with a multi-owned car though, the service history is sometimes supplied, so at least you know where you are putting your hard earned cash!

Unless you are offered a vehicle at a low price for the year, steer well clear of dented vehicles or ones that have, perhaps, lost their shine as the mechanics may have been equally neglected. (And repair prices are not cheap).
It is also easy for the put-it-right-when-it-goes-wrong owners to forget to check any of the numerous oil levels on the underside of the vehicle.
Remember, once a secondhand car has been bought privately,

there is no comeback if it goes wrong.

Garage deals can be better, since at least sometimes they offer a parts and labour guarantee should the vehicle fail. There is no 'special' place to look for secondhand Range Rovers, but it is recommended to look at least at a selection before purchasing.

Models Available

SERIES ONE: June 1970 to Jan 1973.
SERIES TWO: Jan 1973 to Nov 1979.
SERIES THREE: Nov 1979 to June 1984.
LATEST MODEL: June 1984 to date.
FOUR-DOOR MODEL: July 1981 to date.
AUTOMATIC MODEL: August 1982 to date.
FIVE-SPEED MODEL: July 1983 to date.
DIESEL MODEL: April 1986 to date

I have divided up Range Rover production into three main series:

Series One (1970 – 1972)
Range Rovers were produced in a rather spartan form for the first three years with no option of trim. Seat facings were finished in PVC only and there was not even a carpet to be seen anywhere. A far cry from production models today! The headlining was PVC backed with glass fibre and instrumentation was sparse. Other than the instruments housed in the speedo pod, there was only a clock mounted on the left side of the centre dash. Initially, there was not even the option of a rear wipe wash system (later models had one as standard from January 1973) so many models for sale

will not be equipped as such, and similarly, a heated rear window was not standardised until late 1973. Most potential customers are put off because of the above reasons and because the earliest vehicles came without power-assisted steering. However, it must not be overlooked that most of the earliest vehicles on the road today have had various extras attached to them over the years, so some can actually represent very good value for money. One special point: PVC seats get very cold in the winter and extremely hot in the summer, not helped by the large glass area of the non-tinted windows! Because of this, they can crack very easily, so seat covers (if fitted) are worth looking under to see what they are covering.

Series Two (1973 – 1979)

Usually the most sought after, Series Two cars bridge the gap between expensive newer models and the spartan older models. Most Series Two cars come with tinted windows and cloth seats, (an option until 1979), and all have more sound insulation than the earliest cars. Creature comforts started arriving in 1973, so all cars in this series have cigar lighters and carpeted transmission tunnels.

However, from about 1975, the insurance group increased to group five resulting in higher premiums for essentially the same car. Nearing the end of the lifespan of the Series Two, overdrive became a welcome option in 1978, proving a new way to save fuel.

Series Three (1979 – 1984)

Series Three models were better equipped, with crushed velour upholstery (from March 1980) and more luxurious interior appointments. The bonnet and (especially) the tailgate do not rust as fast, as transfer strip badging replaced the old plastic letter badging that needed holes drilled to keep them in place. All Series Three cars should have

carpeting, tinted windows, cloth seats and power-assisted steering as standard. However, from July 1981, the Range Rover changed from two star petrol to four star, due to the increase in compression ratio.

CLUBS, SPECIALISTS & BOOKS

Clubs

Despite the fact that there are now well over 150,000 Range Rovers world wide, there is only one club dealing exclusively with the marque. Certainly there are several four-wheel drive type groups that cover a wide spectrum of vehicles. However, in the UK the only club is the Range Rover Register, which was formed at the beginning of 1985. The address of the secretary is:

Jonathan Rogers,
The Range Rover Register,
The Cottage,
Castle Mill,
Goldington Road,
BEDFORD MK41 0JA.
Tel: 0234-62441

The original aim of the club was to deal just for the earliest vehicles ('H' registered) but due to the overwhelming amount of interest caused it was decided to deal with vehicles of all years. Some of the activities proposed for the club at the inaugural meeting in early 1985 were: Caravanning/camping; competitive events; green roading; restoration/maintenance and motoring festivals. Certainly membership has grown very well

indeed since the start, and the club has now been recognised within the National Association of Rover Clubs Ltd.

Specialist Suppliers

There are a number of specialist coachbuilders who have started to deal with Range Rovers within the past few years, but I have decided not to deal with them in this section since nearly all their work gets exported to such places as the Far East at amazingly high prices often as much as four times the original price of the vehicle.

Most, if not all parts for Range Rovers can be ordered over the counter at BL/Unipart establishments at reasonable cost. However they are not always in stock, and could take a few days/weeks to arrive, just when your vehicle has been branded 'off the road'. The following suppliers boast nationwide delivery usually within return of post.

Simmonites
755 Thornton Road,
Thornton,
Bradford BD13 3NW
Tel: 0274 833351 & 834306

Gill Land Rover Services,
Adamsez,
West Industrial Estate
Scotswood,
Newcastle
Tel: 091 2742868

For replacement panels:
Abercorn Steel Products,
Burnsall Road,
Canley
Coventry
CV5 6BU
Tel: 0203 77041 or 711764

For sales, servicing, body parts, etc:

Candols,
Bansons Yard,
High Street,
Ongar,
Essex
Tel: 0277 364205

Books

Although not dealing exclusively with Range Rover models, the following books prove a worthwhile addition to the Range Rover enthusiasts' library:

The Rover Story by G. Robson (Patrick Stephens). The history of all Rover cars. Not many pictures of Range Rovers, but a reasonable written section on the model. Now in its third edition.
Land Rover, The Unbeatable 4X4 by K.&J. Slavin & G.N. Mackie (Haynes/Foulis). Very successful and now in its second edition. Lots of good information on the preparation of safaris. The reprinted edition has been fully updated.
The Hundred Days of Darien by Russell Braddon (Collins). Although by now well out of print (1974), this book gives a fascinating account of the Darien Gap section of the 1971-1972 British Trans Americas expedition. Well worth the search.
Where the Trails Run Out by John Blashford-Snell. Another long out of print publication covering the BTAE expedition written by the leader of the expedition.

The following books deal almost exclusively with the Range Rover:
Range Rover 1970-1981 (Brooklands Books). Another book in the Brooklands series, covering road and long term test features etc., from mostly British contemporary magazines. A must for the enthusiast who missed the reports first time round.
Range Rover/Land Rover by G. Robson (David & Charles). From the same author as *The Rover Story* this book is now celebrating its second print. It contains some behind-the-scenes stories of design and development, but most of the photographs have appeared before.

Range Rover Companion by Stuart Bladon (Kimberleys). This, the most recently published of those listed, covers some previously unpublished points on the design and production. It contains many photographs taken at Eastnor Castle grounds where BL test their Range Rovers in arduous conditions. The book also has an interesting motorsport photographic section.

Range Rover Owners Workshop Manual (Haynes Publishing). A step-by-step guide on maintenance, engine and body stripping, and rebuilding. Has the added advantage over the factory manual, having photographs. Each Haynes manual is produced after stripping down a complete vehicle, so any problems encountered are highlighted. The book is a must for DIY owners.

Autobooks manual Another DIY car maintenance book this time making extensive use of line drawings. Not as popular as the Haynes publication.

BL Factory Workshop Manual For several years, the only workshop manual available on the model, it has been updated and reprinted several times to keep it in line with current models. Only disadvantage is that it often tells the reader to make use of specialist tools only available from Rover dealers, when other, cheaper ones, might do the job equally well.

PHOTO GALLERY

1. Thirteen of the first series of Road Rovers were built in the 50s. Like this sole known survivor, pictured in 1985, most were two-wheel drive. (Photo by David Shephard)

2. Eleven of the Series 2 Road Rover prototypes were built in the late 50s. This is one of two known survivors and is pictured in 1985 when it was located in London. It has since been purchased by an enthusiast for restoration. (Photo by David Shephard)

3. One of the batch of 25 pre-production Range Rovers photographed in early 1970. YVB 153H and YVB 160H (not shown here) were the first two vehicles completed in this batch, for photographic use in the earliest pamphlet and publicity shots. Note the Rover emblem embossed in the wheel centres. This idea was not carried forward on to production vehicles. (Courtesy Tony Hutchings)

4. Note the unpainted alloy trailing edge of the sliding window. This was painted black on production models until 1974, when it was omitted altogether. Naturally the 'family' who appeared in advertising shots with YVB 153H were models! (Courtesy Tony Hutchings)

5. Note the long jack handle extension mounted on the bottom of the folded rear seat. The 'corrugated rubber' flooring was replaced by a flat PVC covering in October 1973. (Courtesy Tony Hutchings)

6 and 7. Although shown here in pre-production form, the interior of the earliest Range Rovers was equally spartan. It remained this way until January 1973 when carpet was added to the transmission tunnel, and October 1973 with the introduction of optional cloth seats. (Courtesy Tony Hutchings)

8

9

10

11

12

8. Early press vehicles lined up outside the Meudon Hotel near Falmouth for the press launch in early June 1970. Twenty vehicles plus a rolling chassis were present, and the launch was spread over three days (Courtesy Tom Barton)

9. Gentlemen of the press enjoy a chat on the hotel patio. Note the cut-down rolling chassis on display, and the well polished standard vehicle. (Courtesy Tom Barton)

10. The press were able to assess the incredible hill climbing abilities of the new vehicle, up the steep sides of Blue Hills mine, near St. Agnes, Cornwall. In the background lies Trevaunance Cove. NXC 243H stands in the foreground. (Courtesy Tom Barton)

11. Still on the steep sides of Blue Hills mine, an early press vehicle makes the steep ascent. Note the early-style screw-off petrol cap on the left. This is Geoff Miller at the helm of NXC 235H. (Courtesy Tom Barton)

12. Geoff Miller demonstrates to the press, the tremendous power of the vehicle. (Courtesy Tom Barton)

13. VXC 757K was one of the two Range Rovers used on the 1971-2 Alaska-Cape Horn British Trans Americas Expedition. This vehicle has been extensively rebuilt since the expedition, although the other car (VXC 868K) has remained largely untouched. (Colin Pearce)

14. In action in the jungle aboard the Avon 'floating bridge'. (Photo via David Shephard)

13

14

15

17

18

16

19

20

15. Earliest pre-production models carried metal letter badges instead of plastic ones. YVB 175H (shown here) still survives with its metal badges.

16. Until 1973, these shorter, squarer-profile badges were fitted to the deck panels of the vehicle. Photograph no. 23 shows the revised type, introduced to alleviate problems with undergrowth getting lodged between the badge and the bodywork.

17. Pete Hutchings' vehicle, SXC 237M, parked at an angle of about 37°, showing that the centre of gravity is quite low. Pete, however, had to climb out from the passenger door! The vehicle will park on a 45° slope.

18. The chassis number from the same vehicle shows that the vehicle was originally intended for the export market. Indeed, the vehicle was registered by the factory as it carries 'XC' in the registration plate.

19. The rear lamps remained like this until 1979, when mandatory fog lamps were incorporated within the unit itself.

20. The large indicator/side lamp clusters on the front of the vehicle. Many owners cover these with optional light guards for protection in arduous conditions.

21. Under the bonnet of a 1974 example. This car was built shortly before the air filter intake tube was changed from round to square profile.

22. The 'By Land Rover' badge was discontinued in the 1979 improvements, along with the Range Rover side motifs.

23. The later type side motif (1973–1979) was smoother than the earlier type and was also a few millimetres longer. The previously recessed lettering was now merely painted on.

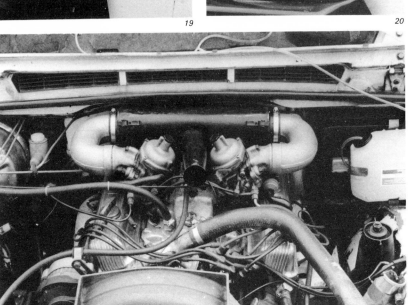

21

22

23

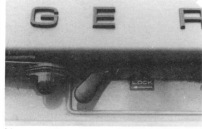

24

25

26

27

28

24. The plastic lettering was replaced in 1979 by transfer strip badging. Note the small 'lock' label to the right of the handle, that cannot be ordered over the parts counter! Its ommission can often tell a replacement bottom tailgate!

25. Bonnet-mounted mirrors remained a standard fitting until the advent of optional door mirrors in 1977, and were actually discontinued in favour of the latter in 1979. The mirror surround was plastic, and the stalk was metal.

26. The three-spoke steering wheel was another part which lasted until 1979, when a thicker rimmed four-spoked type replaced it.

27 & 28. The second type of vinyl seat, a replacement of the type shown in photo 5. This type of seat facing is rarer as most customers ordered their vehicles with cloth seat facings by this time, but in fact, vinyl seats have generally proved more hard wearing. Note the twin seat tip mechanisms, which were incorporated into the front seats in January 1973.

29

30

29. The same 1975 vehicle shown from the rear. Note that the floor covering is different from the corrugated rubber type of the earliest vehicles. Note the seat release lever.

30. With the rear seat in position, there are 36 cubic feet of usable stowage space, but with the seats tipped down, this increases to 71 cubic feet!

31. The two tailgates open wide at the rear allowing easy entry to the large boot. The top tailgate is held up by two pneumatic struts fixed to the upper rear three-quarter panels. Note the hinged number plate (discontinued in 1984) to allow legal use of the lowered tailgate.

31

32

33

34

35

36

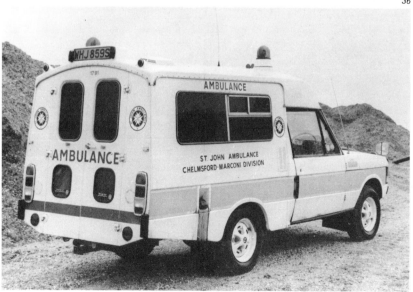

37

38

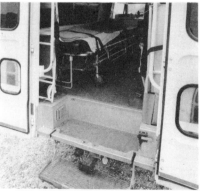

39

32. Note the ground clearance, shown quite clearly here. There is clearance of about 12 inches under the body, and 7¹/₂ inches under each of the two differentials. The Range Rover has beam axles rather than independent suspension, as the latter would seriously affect the vehicle's off-road capabilities.

33. The first cloth seats were available from October 1973 (vehicles carrying 'M' suffix registration in GB) and inertia-reel safety belts were offered as an option from that time.

34. The same type of seat facings shown in the rear. Four adults can be carried easily in ample comfort; the interior width is 66 inches.

35. Many owners have updated their vehicles by painting the bumpers black, as this was standardised by the factory in 1979. Previous to this time, they were painted aluminium.

36. The very first Range Rover ambulance was based upon YVB 158H and is now owned by Worcester Red Cross. This is a 1977 Wadham Stringer based ambulance and is owned by St. John Ambulance, Marconi Division, Chelmsford.

37. The vehicle has a 10-inch chassis extension and an extra 12 inch rear overhang. The rear bodywork is fibre-glass.

38. The cab of the Wadham Stringer ambulance. Note that the seat facings are black. Note also the large emergency lights/siren operation pod mounted on the middle of the dash top.

39. A flip-down step is mounted on the rear of the vehicle which is equipped with three front-facing seats and a stretcher.

40

41

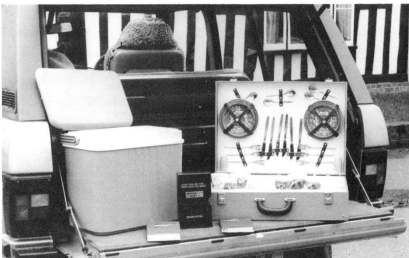

42

43

44

45

46

40. By 1979, vehicles were fitted with revised rear lamp clusters that incorporated compulsory (to GB) fog lamps. The bumpers were also painted black.

41. The Range Rover Vogue was launched in early 1981 and was finished in its own special colour – Vogue Blue. This model was an up-market version of the standard vehicle and had twin side stripes as standard.

42. There were 250 Vogues built for the UK market and all were equipped with a special picnic hamper in matching trim. Note also the Range Rover cool box on display.

43. Air conditioning was offered for the first time with the Vogue model. The outlet vents can be seen along the length of the dashboard in this photograph. Note the post-1979 type, four-spoke steering wheel.

44. This seat facing was introduced in March 1980, and superseded the earlier type of cloth seats shown in photos 33 & 34. The headrests had separate pop-off cushions in matching trim.

45. Wood door cappings were fitted to Vogue models as standard equipment, and the door lower trims were faced with brushed velour to match the seats.

46. The side sliding window catch shown on a 1981 model. Note the holes drilled in the channel so that the window can be fixed into position.

47

48

49

50

47. Central wheel motifs were added to the luxurious specification of the Vogue, to further enhance its appearance.

48. Part of a 1981 model toolkit. This fixes to the inside of the off-side rear wing, immediately behind the wheel arch. A foot pump is standard.

49. Bull bars and light guards certainly not only improve the looks, but also protect the lights. This photo may look set up, but Bill King genuinely did bash the front of his car immediately before the picture was taken!

50. In July 1981 (at the launch of the four-door model) alloy wheels were made optional. They carried the same tyres, however.

51

52

53

51. The original four-door model. Note the reduced size front quarter-light windows that looked more aesthetically pleasing with the reduced size front doors. The door locks were later incorporated into the handles in 1983, with the introduction of the five-speed gearbox.

52. Larger door mirrors were fitted in the June 1984 improvements. These are on a Vogue model and are electronically operated and heated.

53. Latest models have an underbonnet inspection lamp as standard. The light is activated when the bonnet is opened.

54

57

59

61

55

58

60

62

56

54. Note the lack of hinged rear number plate on a 1985 model. New rear number plate lights are mounted on the bottom tailgate.

55. Headlamp jet washers were added to the specification in 1984. The halogen headlamps were standardised from 1979.

56. The latest dashboard layout, as from June 1984. The four dials previously on the centre dash were discontinued and incorporated in the larger speedo pod.

57. The odometer had an extra digit added in 1984, and the possible reading increased to 999,999 miles! A rev counter was also made standard.

58. The 1984 specification four-door front seats reclined for the first time. Note the fold down armrests and new door pillar-mounted height-adjustable safety belts.

59. Models built with air conditioning have no space for a glovebox, and so one is mounted on the transmission tunnel between the front seats. Note the electric window switches.

60. The petrol cap was revised from screw-off to flip up in 1973. This is one fitted to a 1985 vehicle. The side rubbing strips are factory approved extras.

61. Very soft suspension and heavy payloads often mean sagging springs after a few years. In this line-up, not two vehicles seem to sit at the same height!

62. A converted six-wheeler car. This one belongs to BBC Radio 1 and is used for towing their large trailer for roadshows. (Gary Smith)

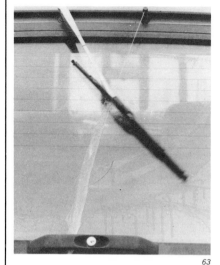

63

64

65

66

67

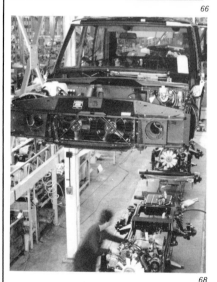

68

69

70

71

63. A rear wipe wash was added to the vehicle's specification in January 1973. The water is carried via plastic piping through from the front water bottle, which also fed the front window jets.

64. On all but the pre-production cars, Range Rovers were fitted with this warning plate at the centre bottom of the dash.

65. A new four door model, poses alongside pre-production vehicle no YVB 175H which is left-hand drive. This has chassis number 35800002A. Note that the overall shape of the vehicle has not changed at all.

66. The engine from the October 1985 fuel injection vehicle developed 165 bhp @ 4750 rpm, the most powerful factory Range Rover.

67. The October 1985 Vogue model featured twin quartz halogen spotlamps on an all new detachable polyurethane front spoiler. At the same time, the vehicle saw new side body rubbing strips, complete with chrome finish. New tyres also had to be developed, to cater for the increase of 10 mph in the top speed.

68. 1985 vehicles under construction. The body is still lowered down onto the chassis and running gear, but note the new all-welded construction replacing the previously bolted together panels.

69. The only external change to the new diesel is the Turbo D badge on the tailgate. (Courtesy of David Shephard)

70. This rather battered Range Rover is competing in a timed cross-country event with Britain's All Wheel Drive Club. It is often the Range Rover based vehicles that take top honours.

71. When it retired from the streets, this Range Rover found a new life in competition with the All Wheel Drive Club. The added roll-cage is an essential safety requirement of the club.